Rethinking the Ontological Argument
A Neoclassical Theistic Response

In recent years, the ontological argument and theistic metaphysics have been criticized by philosophers working in both the analytic and continental traditions. Responses to these criticisms have primarily come from philosophers who make use of the traditional, and problematic, concept of God. In this volume, Daniel A. Dombrowski defends the ontological argument against its contemporary critics, but he does so by using a neoclassical or process concept of God, thereby strengthening the case for a contemporary theistic metaphysics. Dombrowski builds on Charles Hartshorne's crucial distinction between divine existence and divine actuality, which enables neoclassical defenders of the ontological argument to avoid the familiar criticism that the argument moves illegitimately from an abstract concept to concrete reality. His argument, thus, avoids the problems inherent in the traditional concept of God as static.

Daniel A. Dombrowski is professor of philosophy at Seattle University. He is the author of fourteen books and more than one hundred scholarly articles, and he has written broadly in the area of process or neoclassical theism.

D1566591

Rethinking the Ontological Argument

A Neoclassical Theistic Response

DANIEL A. DOMBROWSKI

Seattle University

CAMBRIDGE UNIVERSITY PRESS
Cambridge, New York, Melbourne, Madrid, Cape Town,
Singapore, São Paulo, Delhi, Tokyo, Mexico City

Cambridge University Press
32 Avenue of the Americas, New York, NY 10013-2473, USA

www.cambridge.org
Information on this title: www.cambridge.org/9780521326353

First published 2006
First paperback edition 2011

A catalog record for this publication is available from the British Library

Library of Congress Cataloging in Publication data
Dombrowski, Daniel A.
Rethinking the ontological argument : a neoclassical theistic response /
Daniel A. Dombrowski.
p.   cm.
Includes bibliographical references (p.   ) and index.
ISBN 0-521-86369-4 (hardback)
1. Theism.   2. Process theology.   3. God – Proof, Ontological.   1. Title.
BD444.D67   2006
212′.1–dc22   2004028311

ISBN 978-0-521-86369-8 Hardback
ISBN 978-0-521-32635-3 Paperback

Contents

Acknowledgments

I am extremely grateful to Donald Viney and to an anonymous reader from Cambridge University Press for insightful comments on an earlier version of this book. Likewise, I am appreciative of comments I have received from faculty and students at Johan Wolfgang Goethe University in Frankfurt (especially Thomas Schmidt), as well as from faculty and students at two universities in Poland: University of Silesia and Catholic University of Lublin (especially Piotr Gutowski). The chapter on Rorty has been improved as a result of criticisms from various members of the Society for the Advancement of American Philosophy; likewise the chapter on Taylor has benefited from criticisms by various members of the Society for the Study of Process Philosophy. Much of Chapter 2 appears in an article of mine in volume 38 of *Metaphilosophy* and much of Chapter 3 is based on an article in volume 21 of *American Journal of Theology & Philosophy*. I have also learned much from a public debate on the ontological argument I had at Seattle University with James Reichmann.

Introduction

Three key moments in the history of the ontological argument can be identified. First, in the eleventh century St. Anselm stated the argument in an explicit way for the first time, or at least one could argue that this is the case. Second, in the eighteenth century the criticisms of the ontological argument by Hume and Kant struck what seemed to be the death knell of the argument. And third, in the middle decades of the twentieth century several thinkers – most notably Charles Hartshorne, Norman Malcolm, and John Findlay – breathed new life into the argument by claiming that Hume and Kant criticized only the weaker version of the ontological argument, found in Ch. 2 of Anselm's *Proslogion*, not the stronger modal version, found in Ch. 3. To be precise, Hartshorne is the one who discovered two versions of the argument in Anselm's *Proslogion* in 1953 (see Hartshorne 2000, 96–97). Seven years later Malcolm wrote his justly famous article (Malcolm 1960). Further, Hartshorne was the first to give a formalized version of the argument using the calculus of modal logic (Hartshorne 1961b; 1962, 50–51).

The present book is an attempt to assess the impact of this third key moment in the history of the ontological argument on contemporary philosophy. I should be clear at the outset that I think there are several versions of the ontological argument – both in ordinary language and formal versions – that are not only valid but sound. Further, I think that Hartshorne's version of the ontological argument (rather than, say, Malcolm's) is especially worthy of defense. But I will not be examining in detail the debates among Hartshorne, Malcolm, and Findlay themselves, nor between these thinkers taken as a group and their various critics in the mid- and late-twentieth century. Rather, I will be putting

1

a Hartshornian defense of the ontological argument in dialectical tension with six different scholars who have more recently written on the
argument.

Chapters 2 and 3 deal with English-language thinkers who are skeptical of the ontological argument, in particular, and of metaphysical arguments, in general, from what can be designated as a "continental" point
of view (mixed with a neopragmatist point of view, in one case). Chapter 2 deals with a lifelong debate between Hartshorne and one of his most
illustrious pupils: Richard Rorty. I will contrast Hartshorne's defense of
metaphysics and of the ontological argument with Rorty's preference for
"poetry," as he uses the term. Indeed, Rorty thinks that poets should
replace both metaphysicians and scientists as the leaders of culture.

Chapter 3 deals with Mark Taylor, a very influential deconstructionist
thinker who has both examined in detail and taken swipes at the ontological argument. A critical engagement with Taylor's thought will bring
to the surface the rather expansive use of apophatic discourse that is
characteristic of many contemporary philosophers of religion influenced
by continental thought, especially by Jacques Derrida. I will argue that
an overuse of negative theology is not as humble as it first appears, but
rather constitutes an overly muscular use of a certain positive (and, I
allege, mistaken) view of God that is monopolar.

The fourth and fifth chapters of the book deal with an analytic philosopher who has written the most careful, detailed (indeed, encyclopedic!)
criticism of the ontological argument: Graham Oppy. As with Rorty and
Taylor, Oppy develops certain criticisms of the ontological argument, in
general, and of Hartshorne's version of it, in particular, that are telling.
Nonetheless, his nuanced "general objection" to the ontological argument is, I argue, defective precisely because it ignores a key distinction
in Hartshorne between existence and actuality. I will show that by assuming the simple dichotomy between essence and existence, it is too easy
for Oppy to push through his criticisms of the ontological argument.
The more complex trichotomy of essence-existence-actuality, however,
enables a defender of the ontological argument to escape Oppy's general objection.

Despite Oppy's facility with modal logic, he does not deal primarily
with formal versions of the ontological argument, but rather with ordinary language versions (Oppy 1995, 3). I will follow him in this regard.
Obviously I do not want to be interpreted as being content with unnecessary vagueness or ambiguity (nor does Oppy). Rather, along with Edgar
Towne, I wish to claim that in the formulation of a defensible version of

the ontological argument there is still a great need for informal clarification of concepts and discovery. The clarification and discovery that will become evident in the present book could no doubt be "translated" into (or better, be "mapped" onto) a formal language; in fact, Hartshorne himself offers a formal version of his argument. I am assuming here that a formal version of the ontological argument is at least compatible with the flux of events and concepts that are involved in the hard work of constructing an ordinary language version of the argument.

Further, I hope to show that a defense of the ontological argument does not make the case for the necessary existence of God an exception to logical principles. When I claim at different points in the book that God is exceptional, this exceptional status will be the conclusion of an effort at rational argumentation, not an evasion of such (Towne, 1999, 241–243; Hartshorne 1941, 301). As Hartshorne puts the point: "Anselm's Principle seems to be vindicated. Greatness is conceivable only as existent, by the very criteria which allow us to conceive either the existence or the nonexistence of any island, dollar, devil, you please" (Hartshorne 1965, xiii, 65, 71).

My treatment of Oppy's views will lay bare what I take to be a significant contribution made by Hartshorne to the rationality of religious belief. At the one extreme are those who strip theistic belief of intellectual content. This extreme includes both unbelievers, who are convinced that theistic belief is epistemologically impoverished, as well as fideists, who are content with a faith that either transcends reason altogether or is meant to replace it. Among these fideists are those who deemphasize Anselm's ontological argument or who deny its existence by claiming that Anselm's *Proslogion* is an extended *prayer* rather than an intellectual attempt to argue for something. On this view the ontological "argument" is only a memorable part of that prayer (e.g., Moore 2003, 32).

At the other extreme are those who see the ontological argument as just one more deductive argument on a par with all others such that the chain of argumentation in it is only as strong as its weakest link. Many of the formal versions of the ontological argument that were presented in the wake of the Hartshorne, Malcolm, Findlay renaissance of the argument exhibit this tendency (e.g., Nasser and Brown 1969). The problem with this extreme view is not so much that the ontological argument is over-intellectualized as that the type of rationality used seems too restrictive, given the intellectual task. It seems that very few people can be persuaded or coerced into believing in the existence of God by deductive argument alone, with its "take it or leave it" character.

Hartshorne's contribution lies somewhere between these extremes, and this is so for two reasons. First, although he is firmly committed to the task of rationally justifying belief in God, he does not think that any one argument, not even the ontological one, is sufficient. That is, he rejects the (Kantian) metaphor of an argument only being as strong as its weakest link and prefers instead the (Peircian) one to the effect that when several arguments mutually reinforce each other the common conclusion of these arguments is made stronger, as in the mutually reinforcing strands that make up a cable. Recent critics of the ontological argument have largely ignored the context of the ontological argument in a larger, cumulative, global argument where the weaknesses of any one argument are compensated by the strengths in other arguments, the testimony of religious experience, and so on, as was also the case in Duns Scotus (see Viney 1985, 10–11). Of course each of the argument strands in the cable must be valid: six invalid arguments do not mutually reinforce any conclusion worth believing.

As Donald Viney has aptly put the point, Hartshorne has rightly abandoned the notion that there could be a *demonstration* of God's existence if this means that there could be a deductively sound argument that every rational agent would accept. The use of position matrices enables one to steer a moderate course between a purely logical or deductive approach in relation to the question of God's existence, on the one hand, and a purely subjective or fideistic approach based solely on preference or faith, on the other.

Second, although Hartshorne himself offered a formal, deductive version of the ontological argument (Hartshorne 1962, 49–57), his more usual procedure is to work from position matrices so as to lay out the logically possible options to a particular problem, which in this case deals with the relationships among necessity-contingency and God's existence-nonexistence. Each option is carefully examined to determine its strengths and weaknesses. In effect, a defender of the Hartshornian version of the ontological argument forces one to be explicit regarding the price one is willing to pay in such a defense in that one has to confront the atheistic, agnostic, or positivist options. Likewise, the point to this type of defense of the ontological argument is to require the unbeliever to do the same regarding the plausibility of the theist's case, contra the all-or-nothing character of simple deduction. Deduction is part of a larger dialectical whole, on the Hartshornian view, a fact that is very much relevant when responding to Oppy's charge that the ontological argument is not dialectically effective.

Whereas Chapters 2 through 5 deal with three thinkers who ultimately reject the ontological argument, Chapter 6 deals with three defenders of the ontological argument: Thomas Morris, Katherin Rogers, and Alvin Plantinga. But these three thinkers defend not only Anselm's argument for the existence of God, but also Anselm's *concept* of God. I will argue that classical theism, even an Anselmian version of classical theism, is problematic for several reasons and therefore that the traditional (and unsolvable) problems found in classical theism have led many thinkers to prematurely reject the ontological argument itself. That is, I will argue that Hartshorne's neoclassical concept of God is more likely than is a classical theistic concept to sustain Anselm's best insights regarding the necessity of God's existence.

Much of the book deals with Oppy's criticisms of the ontological argument. He states: "I conclude that ontological arguments are completely worthless. While the history and analysis of ontological arguments makes for interesting reading, the critical verdict of that reading is entirely negative" (Oppy 1995, 199). There is a clear need for a book that responds in detail to Oppy's influential assessment.

I hope to show that the ontological argument is worth a great deal. First, it provides an effective strategy in the effort to demonstrate the rationality of theism when the theist is in dialectical exchange with unbelievers (e.g., Rorty, Oppy, and in a different way Taylor). Second, it is crucial for theists themselves in their effort to rationally understand what the necessary existence and contingent actuality of God entail. Third, it is an exercise in logic that can be used when confronted by the challenge posed by misologists (e.g., Rorty and Taylor). Fourth, it can be used in such a way as to help clarify the concept of God – the logic of perfection – when dealing with classical theists (e.g., Morris, Rogers, and Plantinga) as opposed to neoclassical theists. And fifth, it is a helpful argument for those who are interested in bridging the rather wide gap in contemporary philosophy of religion that divides continental thinkers (e.g., Taylor and to a lesser extent Rorty) and analytic philosophers (e.g., Oppy, Morris, Rogers, and Plantinga).

Regarding this last point, we should take seriously the comment of Billy Joe Lucas that "as we now carve up our discipline into its many subdisciplines, any attempt to assess ontological arguments at this stage of our history is now beyond the range of competence of the practitioners of any such subfield" (Lucas 1997, 183). I am not quite as pessimistic as Lucas, although I am not quite ready to say that he is wrong, either. In any event, the present book is an effort to see how much *intra*disciplinary dialogue can go on in philosophy concerning the ontological argument. In this regard I will try to introduce scholars outside of process philosophy to the work of several thinkers who have carefully analyzed the onto-logical argument in recent years, but whose work has not been rebutted (or perhaps even read) by either analytic or continental philosophers. I have in mind first-rate scholars such as George Goodwin, Billy Joe Lucas, George Shields, Edgar Towne, and Donald Viney.

Ironically the chapters are intended to be as self-contained as possible. That is, each chapter could be read independently by those who are interested in only one or a few of the six authors who are criticized. However, a reader of all of the chapters will have a reticulative grasp of how a neoclassical (or, more loosely, a process) theism based on a modal version of the ontological argument fares in relation to several different influential strands in contemporary philosophy of religion.

The ontological argument, as I see it, is *the* metaphysical question seen from a particular angle. Getting clear on whether there is a necessary (divine) existent helps us to understand the status of other existents. Thus, despite the enormous attention this argument has received in the past, it is certainly worth the effort to clarify its status in light of recent developments: Rorty's and Taylor's versions of postmodernism; Oppy's scholarly trashing of the argument with the aid of the razor-sharp skills of contemporary analytic philosophy; and Morris's, Rogers', and Plantinga's recent efforts to use the ontological argument or perfect being theol-ogy in the service of traditional theism. When facing ultimate concerns (death, God), human beings face the twin dangers of maniacal faith, on the one hand, and a despairing cynicism or nihilism, on the other. This book is an attempt to mediate between these extremes (Hartshorne 1965, xii, 24–25, 87).

1

Historical Background

A Brief History up until Anselm

This part of the book will be devoted to putting some flesh on the bones of the three key moments in the history of the ontological argument. The purpose of this history is obviously not to do an exhaustive survey of the historical uses of the argument, nor even to do original historical research of some more attenuated sort. Rather, I would like to sketch a history of the ontological argument so as to set the stage for my treatment of the six contemporary authors who are focus of the present book. As with many other topics in philosophy, current thinking about the onto-logical argument involves historical thinking in that the various concepts employed in discourse about the argument (concepts such as that there is that than which no greater can be conceived, perfection, existence as a predicate, necessity v. contingency, etc.) carry with them rich historical resonances (or baggage).

I should begin, I suppose, with Anselm, but there is good reason to think that although he was the first to state the argument explicitly, it is implicit in several earlier thinkers: Plato (Johnson 1963; Dombrowski 2005, Ch. 5; Halfwassen 2002; Mesquita 1994; Ceniza 2003), Philo and the Neoplatonists (Beckaert 1967; Oppy 1995, 101–105, 274–275), Avicenna (Rescher 1960; Morewedge 1970), and others. Oppy does not find the claim that there are implicit versions of the ontological argu-ment in these earlier thinkers very convincing (Oppy 1995, 4; Esser 1905; Barnes 1972), so perhaps a few words in defense of the claim are in order.

Consider the famous divided line of Book Six of Plato's *Republic*. The divided line establishes an epistemological, metaphysical hierarchy "whose supreme rule is that verification is always from above, never from below" (Eslick 1982, 21). The opposite procedure (from below) is exemplified by early logical empiricists like Russell and Carnap, whose reductive analysis of compound sentences terminates in protocol sentences (denoting the sensory atoms of Hume) like "red here."

For example, the lowest level of the divided line is *eikasia*, which is usually translated as "imagination." The objects of such an operation clearly are images, but Plato indicates that these objects are not verified from below, in empiricist fashion, for if they were so verified universal skepticism would result, due to the fleeting character of images. The next highest level is *pistis* or "belief" (which, together with *eikasia*, exhausts the world of *doxa* or "mere opinion" concerning becoming). It is easy to misunderstand the character Socrates (Plato's presumed spokesperson) here. In fact, Plato's own language abets this possible misunderstanding. One gets the impression that the objects of *pistis* are sensible things, which might lead some to mistakenly assume a perceptual realism that is foreign to Plato. Beliefs at this level of the divided line are not so much about the data of the senses as they are about the causes of such effects. As Leonard Eslick insightfully puts the point:

The beliefs we form even about the physical world are trans-empirical.... Their truth or falsity must be determined on a higher level still. In any case the physical feelings ("events" would be more accurate, since for Plato, with his Heraclitean heritage from Cratylus, the physical world is in process) are themselves only images, moving images of eternal [or better, everlasting] spiritual realities. (Eslick 1982, 23)

In order to confirm or falsify beliefs, one needs to do so from above, on the evidence of the divided line passage of the *Republic*. That is, one needs to cross over from the world of becoming to the world of being, as known by way of *dianoia* or "hypothetical understanding." Thinking by way of hypotheses is primarily exemplified for Plato by the mathematical sciences. The necessities discussed and demonstrated in these sciences remain hypothetical, involving an if-then connection in which the "if" clause cannot be eliminated. Further, dianoetic scientific demonstration can be either synthetic (where one begins with the first principles of the sciences – definitions, common notions, postulates – then moves downward deductively to theorems) or analytic (where instead of moving from hypothetical cause to effect, one moves in the reverse direction from effects to hypothetical cause).

To use Eslick's language, the base metals of synthesis and analysis on the level of *dianoia* are transmuted into the gold of *noesis* by an intellectual intuition of the form of the good in Book 7 (Eslick 1982, 27). If one has had such an intuition, the hypotheses of the mathematical sciences are destroyed in the sense that they lose their hypothetical character and are seen as necessary consequences of the unhypothetical first principle.

An insightful article by J. Prescott Johnson is helpful at this point. Johnson understands the Platonic principle that verification comes from above, not from below, to amount to an ontological argument for the necessary existence of the form of the good. Although Johnson does not discuss the relationship between the form of the good and God, if there is legitimacy to the Neoplatonic and early Christian view that forms are items in God's mind, then an argument for the necessary existence of the form of the good would, in effect, be an argument for the necessary existence of God (Johnson 1963, 24–34).

On Johnson's interpretation, the supreme formal reality is not to be treated as a mere hypothesis because it is needed as a principle of order for all of the lesser forms. Knowledge of the form of the good requires no assumptions or hypotheses, nor does it rely on the use of images, as *dianoia* does. To use contemporary language, this knowledge is strictly a priori and necessary. No merely contingent existence could be thus known (Hartshorne 1965, 139–140, 149). *Dianoia* is incapable of yielding incorrigible knowledge both because it begins with an unsubstantiated hypothesis and because it relies on at least partially distorting images.

Noesis, however, is a mode of cognition that may *start* from provisional knowledge of the hypothesis, but it ends with: "... certain knowledge of the ultimate principle which exists with necessity. This principle, ultimate and unconditional, Plato calls the 'unhypothesized beginning' – *archen anhypotheton*" (Johnson 1963, 29). The anhypotheton is the form of the good or the sun in the famous similes of the cave and the sun. Unfortunately, no explicit description is given in the *Republic* concerning the process by which *noesis* moves from hypotheses to the anhypotheton, so any effort to understand this transition involves a certain amount of risky scholarly speculation. This is where Johnson is helpful. It is clear that the noetic move *is* a mode of cognition. In the following, Johnson makes it clear why it is appropriate to see the ontological argument implied in Plato:

The anhypotheton, or the unhypothesized, is the unconditioned. But if the anhypotheton is merely and only a conceptual object, an epistemological construct, it is dependent upon conditions. ... Thus the anhypotheton is either nothing at all – not even thinkable – or it is ontologically real as independent of all extraneous conditions, including the conditions of thought. Since, however, the anhypotheton is thinkable . . . it is clear that the anhypotheton is the ontologically real being necessarily existing in its possession of extra-epistemological reality. (Johnson 1963, 31)

My aim here is merely to claim that the ontological argument is implied in Plato. (It is not to confuse, as perhaps Plato and Johnson do, epistemological necessity with ontological necessity. We will see in response to Rorty that if we are lucky enough to gain knowledge of a necessarily existent God, this occasion for knowledge itself is contingent.) It is thus not surprising that most philosophers in the history of the discipline who have been called Platonists have also been defenders of the ontological argument and of the principle that verification is from "above" rather than from "below," as empiricists suggest, by way of contrast. The quotation from Johnson makes it clear that, on a Platonic basis, to claim that the anhypotheton is contingent is a contradiction in terms: to say that the anhypotheton depends for its existence on certain limiting conditions or hypotheses is to contradict oneself.

As Hartshorne repeatedly emphasized throughout his career, on the basis of the ontological argument we can conclude that God's existence (including God's understanding of the form of the good) is either impossible or necessary, as the only remaining alternative in modal logic (i.e., the contingent existence of God) is contradictory regarding the argument that no greater being is conceivable. Hence the argument is best seen as suggesting that *if* God's existence is possible, then it is necessary. Johnson, as can be seen in the passage just quoted, is confident that we *can* have a concept of the form of the good (and, by implication, of God). Hence God is possible, despite the fact that there is evidence in the text (509B) of a certain apophatic tendency in Plato wherein the form of the good transcends essence in dignity and power.

In any event, the cosmological argument in the *Laws* and *Timaeus* can be used to supplement the implicit ontological argument in the *Republic* in the following way. The cosmological argument makes it clear that we *can* get a legitimate concept of God. This concept facilitates the following choice before us as a result of the ontological argument: either God's existence is impossible or necessary; but it is not impossible (as in the cosmological argument); hence it is necessary. The two arguments are thus working in the fashion of the aforementioned mutually reinforcing strands in a (Peircian) cable that lead to an overall or global argument for the existence of God that is quite strong (Hartshorne 1970; Viney 1985; Peikoff 1984). This reading of Plato enables us to see how he might have responded to atheists, who existed even in his day (see *Laws* 885B–D; also Hartshorne 1967a, 125). It also enables us to see a certain continuity not often noticed between Plato and Aristotle. Aristotle is quite clear (*Physics* 203b30) that the eternal cannot be contingent: to be possible and to exist do not differ for an eternal or necessary existent (Hartshorne 1965, 141; 1990, 302).

These Platonic and Aristotelian influences were no doubt in the background of St. Augustine's and Boethius's anticipations of the ontological argument (Hartshorne 1965, 149, 250–251), such as Augustine's definitions of God (*De Libero Arbitrio* VI, 14) as "than whom none is greater" and "than whom nothing is proved to be higher." One major difference between the Platonic anticipations of the ontological argument and any defensible contemporary version of it is that in the latter one must make it clearer than Plato did that our coming to knowledge of the necessary existent is contingent: knowledge *of* necessary existence does not occur necessarily. This will be discussed in Chapter 2.

Anselm

Oppy is correct to note that the first explicit statement of the ontological argument was by Anselm in the eleventh century. It is now generally held, largely due to Hartshorne, that Anselm's short work *Proslogion* contains two quite different versions of the argument. It must be admitted that some scholars still think that Ch. 2 of *Proslogion* contains the main argument and that Ch. 3, as well as Anselm's "Replies to Gaunilo," are mere supplements to the main argument (Stearns 1970; Brecher 1985). Oppy, however, reluctantly follows Hartshorne and others in holding that there are two distinct versions of the ontological argument in *Proslogion* and that these deserve separate treatment. But he does not go as far as some scholars, who take nuanced differences of expression in Anselm to constitute three or even four different versions of the argument (Sontag 1967; Nakhnikian 1967). Two is enough.

The crucial passage from Ch. 2, where the first version is found, is translated by S. N. Deane as follows:

Hence, even the fool is convinced that something exists in the understanding, at least, than which nothing greater can be conceived. For, when he hears of this, he understands it. And whatever is understood, exists in the understanding. And assuredly that, than which nothing greater can be conceived, cannot exist in the understanding alone. For, suppose it exists in the understanding alone: then it can be conceived to exist in reality; which is greater. Therefore, if that, than which nothing greater can be conceived, exists in the understanding alone, the very being, than which nothing greater can be conceived, is one, than which a greater can be conceived. But obviously this is impossible. Hence, there is no doubt that there exists a being, than which nothing greater can be conceived, and it exists both in the understanding and in reality. (Anselm 1982, 8; for the Latin, see Charlesworth 1965, 116)

From the start Oppy is skeptical regarding, first, whether the notion of a being than which no greater can be conceived is coherent, and, second, whether there is good reason to suppose that existing in reality is a great-making property solely in the case of a being than which no greater can be conceived, assuming for the moment that such *can* be coherently conceived (Oppy 1995, 7–11; Schnepf 1998).

These are difficult matters and will be treated in detail in this book. But it should not be assumed at the outset that Hartshorne disagrees with Oppy on the question of whether that than which no greater can be conceived is coherent. At this early point we should be content to notice one of Oppy's formulations of the first version of the argument so as to see how it differs from the second version found in Ch. 3. The Ch. 2 version goes as follows, according to Oppy:

1. One can conceive of a being than which no greater can be conceived (premise).
2. If a being than which no greater can be conceived does not exist, then one can conceive of a being greater than a being than which no greater can be conceived, namely, a being than which no greater can be conceived and that exists (premise).
3. Hence a being than which no greater can be conceived exists (from 1, 2) (Oppy 1995, 109).

Oppy thinks that premise 1 can be reasonably rejected by the atheist or agnostic, and thus the argument fails. Nonetheless Oppy reluctantly admits that some theists (not Hartshorne) might reasonably think that this version of the ontological argument is sound (Oppy 1995, 109–111, 208–212). The tension here indicates in a nutshell why Oppy is an agnostic rather than an atheist.

The crucial passage from Ch. 3 that many believe constitutes a quite different version of the ontological argument is as follows:

And it assuredly exists so truly, that it cannot be conceived not to exist. For, it is possible to conceive of a being which cannot be conceived not to exist; and this is greater than one which can be conceived not to exist. Hence, if that, than which nothing greater can be conceived, can be conceived not to exist, it is not that, than which nothing greater can be conceived. But this is an irreconcilable contradiction. There is, then, so truly a being than which nothing greater can be conceived to exist, that it cannot even be conceived not to exist. (Anselm 1982, 8–9; for the Latin, see Charlesworth 1965, 118)

Hartshorne, Malcolm, and others have championed the view that this is a modal argument in that the claim being made is not that God exists, but that God exists *necessarily*: the mode of God's existence is a real predicate that says something significant about God. This version is quite different from the version of the argument found in Ch. 2, on this interpretation. Oppy goes along with this reading of Anselm, presumably because of the strength of recent scholarly opinion arrayed against him on this point. But ultimately he is not convinced.

Oppy thinks that Anselm was not so much offering an independent version of an argument for the existence of God in Ch. 3 as he was "discovering" one of the attributes of the being whose existence was "proved" in Ch. 2. In any event, it *is* possible, he admits, to choose to present an independent version of the ontological argument on the basis of Ch. 3, and hence he does so. Indeed, Oppy thinks that there are both formal and ordinary language formulations of the second version of the ontological argument found in *Proslogion* that are "undeniably valid" (Oppy 1995, 12–14).

However, Oppy's formulation of the modal version of the ontological argument, found in Ch. 3 of *Proslogion*, strikes even defenders of the ontological argument as weak:

1. It is possible that there is a being than which no greater can be conceived and that necessarily exists (premise).
2. Hence there is a being than which no greater can be conceived and that necessarily exists (from 1) (Oppy 1995, 112).

This ultra-simple formulation of Anselm's second version of the argument, which moves to the conclusion after only one premise, is not as insightful as other formulations offered by scholars.

For example, Viney is very instructive in his reconstruction of the different versions of the argument in Ch. 2 and Ch. 3. He isolates the same number of premises such that one can easily see where the two versions of the argument are similar and where the modal version in Ch. 3 differs from the nonmodal version in Ch. 2. The Ch. 2 version as depicted by Viney looks like this:

1. "God" means "that than which nothing greater can be conceived."
2. The idea of God exists in the mind for "the fool hath said in his heart 'there is no God'" (Psalm 13:1).

3. It is greater to exist in reality and in the mind than to exist in the mind alone.
4. Therefore, if God exists in the mind but not in reality, then God is not the greatest conceivable being.
5. Therefore, God must exist not only in the mind but in reality as well (Viney to Dombrowski; May 6, 2005).

By way of partial contrast, Viney sees the modal version in Ch. 3 in the following terms:

1. "God" means "that than which nothing greater can be conceived."
2. The idea of God is not contradictory.
3. That which can be thought of as not existing (a contingent being) is not as great as that which cannot be thought of as not existing (a necessary being).
4. Therefore, to think of God as possibly not existing (as contingent) is not to think of the greatest conceivable being. It is a contradiction to think of the greatest conceivable being as nonexistent.
5. Therefore, God exists (Viney to Dombrowski; May 6, 2005).

The differences between the two versions of the argument as found in premises 2, 3, and 4 are noteworthy and will be explained throughout the present book.

Also consider Richard Purtill's instructive formulations of both versions of the argument in Anselm, formulations that rely heavily on Hartshorne's use of position matrices so as to lay bare the logically possible options. In the first version we are led, Purtill thinks, to think of four possible combinations:

1. Thought of, existing in reality;
2. Thought of, but not existing in reality;
3. Not thought of, existing in reality;
4. Not thought of, not existing in reality (Purtill 1975, 102; also Baird 1995).

If God is defined as the being such that no greater being is possible, then combinations 3 and 4 can be ruled out almost automatically because the definition itself is evidence that we can in *some* sense think of God. Combination 2 can also be ruled out because if God were merely thought of, but did not exist in reality, then a greater being could be possible. Further, if these four options are an exhaustive list, given the two variables of "thought of" and "existing in reality," then eliminating three of them means that the fourth must be the case.

In Purtill's estimation, this version of the argument is "unconvincing yet *seemingly* irrefutable" (emphasis added) (Purtill 1975, 103). He thinks, along with Oppy *and* Hartshorne, that it can be refuted. On Purtill's (and presumably Oppy's) reasoning, this formulation of the first version of Anselm's argument in Ch. 2 fails in part because all it shows is that *if* the term "God" has any reference, then the reference must be to a really existing being. However, we can deny that the term "God" has any such reference.

It is to be noted that Purtill and Hartshorne (contra Oppy) use the above method of listing position matrices or (more optimistically) logically exhaustive cases so as to eliminate the inadequate ones; the hope is that the meaning of a particular argument is thereby clarified. But both Purtill and Oppy (contra Hartshorne) reject both versions of the ontological argument in Anselm. That is, although Hartshorne rejects the first version in Ch. 2 (for reasons to be discussed later), he accepts the second version in Ch. 3.

Consider Purtill's list of four possible combinations that result from a careful reading of Ch. 3 of *Proslogion*:

1. Existing, and existing necessarily;
2. Existing, but not existing necessarily;
3. Not existing, but not necessarily not existing;
4. Not existing, and necessarily not existing (Purtill 1975, 103–106).

The classic example of the fourth combination is a square-circle, whereas my coffee cup (until now I have always hated coffee, but perhaps my tastes will change) is an example of the third. The newspaper that is at present on my desk, but which is about to be recycled, is an example of the second combination. Is there an example of the first combination? The second version of the ontological argument in Anselm is precisely an attempt to show that there is at least one example of this combination.

Of course in order to connect these four possible combinations of the two variables "existing" and "necessity" to the ontological argument, we need a premise that defines God. Instead of defining God as that than which no greater can be conceived, however, Purtill defines God as a being that exists necessarily. This has the obvious defect of exposing the argument to the charge of begging the question, which is integrally connected to what Oppy calls "*the* general objection" (emphasis added) to all formulations of the ontological argument, as we will see. With a more

suitable (i.e., less question-begging) definition, however, these four possible combinations are very instructive regarding what Anselm's second
version of the ontological argument is all about.

Purtill (along with Oppy) concedes that God does not necessarily not
exist, that God is not impossible like a square-circle, an admission that
permits the elimination of combination 4. If combinations 2 and 3 can
be eliminated, then combination 1 must be the case (again assuming
that the four combinations are logically exhaustive). We will see that
Hartshorne argues in detail for the elimination of combinations 2 and 3
and in the process he avoids begging the question, despite Purtill's and
Oppy's skepticism.

What can be gained from Purtill's (Hartshornian) position matrix formulation of the argument in Ch. 3 of *Proslogion*, in contrast to Oppy's
overly parsimonious formulation with only one premise, is the idea that
if combinations 2 and 3 are considered and eliminated first, then one
can conclude that either God necessarily exists or God necessarily does
not exist and that a valid argument to this effect can be provided (Lewis
1983). Thus, if God exists in any possible world at all then God exists in
all of them in that, whichever way we choose – toward theism or toward
antitheism – the existence of God is not contingent. Once again, Purtill is
not convinced by either version of the ontological argument in Anselm,
but his use of (Hartshornian) position matrices is nonetheless instructive
regarding why some thinkers *are* convinced by the second version of the
argument in Anselm.

From this discussion one may legitimately infer that I interpret
Hartshorne as giving only a conditional defense of Anselm. It is true
that Anselm made a discovery, one of the greatest in the history of philosophy, although he was mistaken as to its nature. Just as Lavoisier made a
great discovery (oxygen), but was mistaken about what it was that he had
discovered (thinking that it was dephlogisticated air), so it is also with
Anselm. The discovery was that, assuming certain (Carnapian) meaning
postulates, the existence of God is necessary, the only alternative to which
is the logical impossibility of God's existence. In other words, the question
of God's existence involves no question of contingent fact. The second
Anselmian version of the ontological argument works against both empirical atheism *and* an exclusively empirical theism.

As Hartshorne puts the issue: "If belief in the divine existence even
makes sense, unbelief does not, and if unbelief makes sense, belief does
not. The issue between them is not one of fact or contingent truth but
of meaning. One side or the other is confused" (Hartshorne 1965, 4,

7–9, 22, 30–31). In the effort to understand perfection (a term that will be discussed further), it is quite relevant to consider that to exist with nonexistence as a conceivable alternative is not a superior mode of existing when contrasted with existing in such a way that there is no possibility of not existing. However, Anselm was not as helpful in the effort to clarify other divine properties besides necessary existence, and herein lies his similarity to Lavoisier. It must also be admitted that Anselm does not employ the terms "necessary" and "contingent" in Chs. 2 and 3 of *Proslogion*. The roughly comparable language he uses in Ch. 3 involves not having the possibility of not existing versus having the possibility of not existing.

The ontological argument does not have to derive the necessary existence of God from faith in such existence. The ontological argument need not be question begging. In order to be able to demonstrate this, it is crucial to note at the outset the difference between the following two sets of contrasts: (1) that which exists in reality as well as in the mind is greater than that which exists in the mind alone (the contrast found in Ch. 2 of *Proslogion*); and (2) that whose nonexistence cannot be conceived is greater than that whose nonexistence can be conceived (the contrast found in Ch. 3 of *Proslogion* as well as in "Replies to Gaunilo" I, V, and IX). The first contrast has had an undue influence on the history of criticism of the ontological argument; the second contrast has received its due only relatively recently, thanks to Hartshorne, Malcolm, and others (see Hartshorne 1965, 11–16, 33–35). There are two modes of existence (necessary and contingent) that must be distinguished in order to understand Anselm's second, modal version of the argument.

On the second version of the argument in Anselm, we need not assume that existence is a predicate, even if attributing necessary existence to God (i.e., existence without conceivable alternative) is to say something informative; it is to predicate something significant about God. Indeed, to exist beyond the reach of contingent circumstances is to exist in a way that is truly remarkable. *Contingent* existence is qualitative, it is a genuine predicate, as is *necessary* existence, even if existence as such is, in a way, neutral, as Kant alleged. There are problems with the simplistic, first version of the argument in Anselm that are avoided in the second version. The first version states, in effect, that existence is good, hence the best conceivable being must have it *extra mentem*, as more than an object of thought. In Anselm's second version of the argument, however, there is no comparison between something that exists and something that does not exist, but rather between two entities that exist, albeit in modally different ways (Hartshorne 1967b, 321–323). Thus, Anselm's great discovery is not to be found in Ch. 2 of *Proslogion*, nor is it to be found in his classical theistic concept of God, as I will show in Chapter 6.

After Anselm

Katherin Rogers may be correct in claiming that the ontological argument is the single most discussed argument in the history of philosophy (Rogers 2000, 1; Hogg 2004). Hence, only the most important moments in the history of the argument after Anselm will be mentioned here, once again to provide the backdrop for the examination of the six contemporary authors who are the subjects of the present book. The most important medieval critic of the argument was no doubt St. Thomas Aquinas. His concern was not, as is sometimes assumed, the separability of essence and existence in God; he readily admits that to have an intuition of God's essence would be to have one as well regarding God's existence. That is, the ontological argument is valid per se or for God, but it is not valid for us, given the fact that we cannot have an intuition of God's essence. Going from the unknown (to us) to the to-be-known is a mistake, he thinks, that could be remedied if we instead, as in the cosmological argument, moved from the known to the provisionally unknown (Hartshorne 1941, 319–320, 334–335).

One may wonder at this point, however, how Aquinas could reach the conclusion he reaches without having already had *some* intuition regarding the essence of God. However, Aquinas is correct to emphasize that if we had a *really* coherent insight into the essence of perfection, we would not only know God's existence, we would also be mystics who would already be contemplatively enjoying divine grace, in which case there would not be much need for an *argument* for the existence of God. To admit this much, however, does not mean that we should attenuate the givenness of the concept of God, as Aquinas does, to the point where the ontological argument is worthless. Our understanding of the logic of perfection, it seems, lies in between mystical knowing and sheer nescience (Hartshorne 1944, 238). It is questionable, to say the least, if Aquinas is correct in claiming that it is impossible for us to conceive of something so great that a greater something cannot be conceived (cf. Brecher 1985, 54).

Although some of the medieval critics of the ontological argument had an awareness of the version in Ch. 3 of *Proslogion*, Aquinas seems to rely entirely on the version in Ch. 2 (*Summa Theologiae* 1a, q. 2, a. 1;

also see *Summa Contra Gentiles* Bk. 1, ch. 10–11). Or better, he seems to think that we must first prove that God exists via the reasoning in Ch. 2 (which he thinks is unlikely), then later move to the idea in Ch. 3 that divine existence is necessary. On this reasoning, by disposing of Ch. 2 one disposes of Ch. 3. This dismissal of the ontological argument is too easy, however. By postponing analysis of the concept of necessary existence, Aquinas postpones a consideration of the stronger Anselmian version of the argument: from the modality "necessity of existence" existence is deducible, but from the modality "contingency of existence" it is not. Nevertheless, Aquinas travels part of the way with Anselm in that he admits that the nonexistence of God is contradictory (Daniels 1909; Hartshorne 1965, 154–163; Rousseau 1980, 24).

But only part of the way. Oppy isolates two different criticisms of the ontological argument in Aquinas. The first amounts to the assertion that there just cannot be a priori claims regarding existence. Oppy tries to rescue this objection from what he sees as Aquinas's poor defense of it in that Aquinas's defense of it, he thinks, is question begging. Oppy's view is that the ontological argument itself is either question begging or invalid. The second criticism of the ontological argument in Aquinas, on Oppy's interpretation, is related to the first: the proposition that God exists has to be a posteriori. Once again, Oppy agrees with this criticism, but he thinks that Aquinas leaves it in a question-begging state. Roughly, the first objection is that it is our inability to comprehend the essence of God that prevents us from reaching a priori knowledge of God's existence. This objection is problematic, however, precisely because what is needed in order to have the ontological argument go through is a comprehension of the abstraction that God is that than which no greater can be conceived: no comprehension of the essence of God beyond this level of understanding is required. Of course to know in concrete detail what it would be like to be that than which no greater can be conceived is quite difficult (Oppy 1995, 122–123, 286–288; Matthews 1963; Davies 1985).

Many medieval philosophers, in addition to Anselm, defended the ontological argument, including Duns Scotus and St. Bonaventure. The latter even shows evidence of having understood the stronger version of the argument in Anselm's Ch. 3 of *Proslogion* and in the "Replies to Gaunilo." Unfortunately, Bonaventure tried in *De mysterio Trinitatis* (I, 1, 29 and V, 48) to improve on the ontological argument by simplifying it so as to say, in effect, that God is God, therefore God exists. This reduces the dialectical worth of the argument to the vanishing point, thereby playing into the hands of an agnostic like Oppy, who claims that the ontological argument is dialectically worthless. It is better, I think, to keep all of the complex factors involved in the ontological argument on the table. This makes it possible for a defender of the argument to bring different factors to the fore when needed, depending on dialectical or rhetorical context (Gilson 1955; Oppy 1995, 5; Hartshorne 1965, 76, 87, 155–156).

Given the previous discussion of the anticipations of the ontological argument in Plato, it is not surprising that the argument flourished among rationalist philosophers in the modern period who were heavily influenced by Plato: Descartes, Leibniz, and Spinoza.

There is considerable disagreement among scholars regarding how many arguments for the existence of God can be found in Descartes' writings and regarding which of these arguments can be called "ontological." James Collins perhaps provides a safe course for us by suggesting that there are at least three arguments for the existence of God in Descartes' *Meditations* (specifically, in "Meditations" III and V), arguments that are also found in other forms in *Discourse on Method, Principles of Philosophy*, and especially *Replies to Objections II*. The first two arguments, on Collins' reading, tend to merge together and the third argument tends to assimilate the previous two. Hence, the ontological argument in some fashion pervades (or infects) all of Descartes' arguments for the existence of God. In fact, the ontological argument in Descartes represents:

... the deepest point of penetration of Cartesian analysis into the significance of human thought. The ultimate meaning of the Cogito is that the ... thinking self shares to some degree in the *divine dynamism* itself, in the *self-affirmation* that is God's distinctive way of being. One becomes aware of this affinity in reflecting upon the import of the clearest and most distinct idea in the mind: the idea of [a] ... perfect being. (Collins 1954, 168)

There are several features of Descartes' use of the ontological argument that are instructive regarding my aim here to champion the ontological argument in the context of contemporary philosophy. First, all of Descartes' arguments for the existence of God work on the connection between essence and existence, a connection that applies only in the case of God's existence. Second, in the *Meditations* Descartes speaks as if existence, in contrast to nonexistence, is a predicate or quality such that to lack it is to fall short of perfection. He thereby appears vulnerable to Kant's critique of the ontological argument. In his replies to his critics (Caterus, Gassendi, and others), however, it is apparent that the key distinction that Descartes would like to make in his use of the ontological argument is between necessary and contingent modes of existence.

This is due to the realization that, even if God exists, if God's existence were accidental then God would not be perfect and hence would not be God. Contingency *of existence* is a limitation. And third, Descartes is helpful when he admits that there is no necessity in our thinking of God, yet when we do so we are necessitated to attribute to God all perfections, especially necessary existence; likewise, we are not necessitated to think of triangles, but when we do so we must attribute to them three-sidedness (Hartshorne 2000, 133–137; Plantinga 1965, 31–49; Dougherty 2002).

Oppy's concern regarding Descartes' use of the ontological argument is the same concern he has with Anselm's and Hartshorne's uses of it: the defender of the ontological argument moves illegitimately from the permissibility of inferring the existence of God on the basis of the onto-logical argument to the conclusion that therefore God exists. That is, ontological arguments typically "discharge an operator." An example of this discharge is when Descartes eliminates the operator "conceive of" in the conclusion (Oppy 1995, 20–23, 113–114, 217–219, 278; Nolan 2001). I will respond to this understandable concern in due course.

Because it was the *Meditations* that were so incredibly influential in the history of philosophy (rather than, say, the *Replies to Objec-tions II*), Descartes unwittingly continued the nonmodal interpretation of the ontological argument, an interpretation that dominated until Hartshorne came on the scene in the twentieth century. This is not sur-prising when it is realized that Descartes, Kant, and many others never actually read Anselm. It was due to the prodding by objectors (especially Gassendi) that Descartes came to his own stronger, modal version of the argument. He provides an admirable example of a philosopher who real-ized his own cognitive imperfection; his very cognizance of degrees of clarity and distinctness led him to some inchoate understanding of an omniscient awareness. (This is in contrast to Hobbes, who, in his objec-tions to Descartes, claimed that we have no idea of God.) Likewise, due to the pressure put on him by his critics, Descartes came to realize that even if the abstraction "nonexistence" is not in itself a defect, contin-gency in an existing thing is. The ontological argument was therefore central to Descartes' development as a dialectician (contra Oppy). Fur-ther evidence of this development is found in the fact that, whereas the ontological argument comes late in the *Meditations* and has a rather minor role there, it is pivotal in the later *Principles of Philosophy*.

Ironically, given the quotation I have given from Collins regarding divine dynamism, we will see that the prime defect in Descartes' treatment of the ontological argument is his unquestioned assumption that the divine, necessary existent has without qualification the classical theistic property of immutability (Collins 1954, 164; Hartshorne 1965, 8, 36, 164–173).

Leibniz follows the Descartes of the *Meditations* in defending the non-modal version of the ontological argument. In his *New Essays Concerning Human Understanding* (and elsewhere), however, he contributes something to the ontological argument not found in Descartes: a possibility premise. Once the contingency of God's existence is ruled out (i.e., Anselm's discovery that contingent existence is at odds with the logic of perfection), we are left with two alternatives: either God's existence is impossible or it is necessary. Hence, if God's existence is possible it is necessary. It is for this reason that attention must be paid to the possible existence of God (Plantinga 1965, 54–56; Adams 1994; Maydole 2003).

There are several senses of "possibility" that must be considered when determining if the existence of God is possible. An elementary sense of the term consists in an absence of internal contradiction. A related sense of the term involves the requirement that the sentence "God exists necessarily" obeys syntactical and semantic rules of language. A third sense of the term involves the violation of no scientific laws. Finally, the possible existence of God involves compossibility with other divine attributes. Regarding this last sense it is noteworthy that Leibniz realized that some things are possible individually, but not together. This realization is crucial in the effort to frame a concept of God when several attributes (concerning power, knowledge, goodness, etc.) are considered together (Lomasky 1970, 252–253; Hartshorne 1941, 321).

Although Leibniz is not clear regarding how these different senses of possibility are related, nor regarding whether all four are required or if they are jointly sufficient, he at least alerts us to the considerations that are involved when one tries to figure out if God's existence is possible (i.e., not impossible). Here we can notice that all of the recent defenses of the ontological argument have said something about the very possibility of God's existence. For example, notice premises 5 and 6 of Malcolm's famous modal formulation of the argument:

1. If God does not exist, God could not come into existence because: (a) if God were caused, or (b) if God just happened to come to exist, God would be a limited being (which is false by definition).
2. If God does exist: (a) God could not have come into existence (see above), nor (b) could God be caused not to exist, for there is

nothing that could cause God to cease existing, nor (c) could God just happen to cease existing.

3. Hence, if God exists, God's existence is necessary.
4. Therefore, God's existence is either necessary or impossible.
5. Only if the concept of God is contradictory or logically absurd could it be impossible.
6. But there is no contradiction or absurdity in the concept of God.
7. Therefore, God necessarily exists (Malcolm 1960, 49; also Lomasky 1970, 258–259).

Malcolm, unlike Descartes, tries to show *why* there is not a contradiction in the concept of a necessarily existing God. Hence, he seems to fulfill Leibniz's demand that the possibility of God's existence be addressed. But by addressing the possibility of God's existence Malcolm does not shift the burden of proof to the defender of the claim that God's existence is possible. Leibniz and Malcolm correctly think that the burden of proof lies with those who deny the logical possibility of deity. Exactly how is the claim that God exists like the existence of a square-circle? (Hartshorne 1965, 200–201).

Leibniz's principle of sufficient reason, which amounts to a sort of ultrarationalism, is not a required part of the ontological argument. This is because there is no sufficient reason for *how* God exists (divine actuality), only a convincing argument *that* God necessarily is (divine existence). Only the bare essence and existence of God, taken as an a priori abstraction, is established as a result of the ontological argument, not the more concrete actuality that specifies how God exists from moment to moment.

Oppy is correct to emphasize Leibniz's improvement over Descartes regarding the coherence of, and hence the possibility of, divine existence. This is an improvement that was already anticipated by Duns Scotus' effort to weed out any contradictions in the concept of God. But Oppy trivializes this improvement when he suggests that consistency in the concept we have about God is not one of the fundamental questions that must be addressed in an evaluation of the ontological argument. If it is correct that the existence of God is either impossible or necessary, how could the question of the possibility of God's existence, in the sense of there being no inconsistency in God's existing, not be a fundamental one? It seems that Oppy is holding out for the alternative that is ruled out by Anselm: that God is contingent. We will be alert in Chapters 4 and 5 to see if

Oppy can explain how the logic of perfection could tolerate the greatest conceivable being having the possibility of passing into or out of existence due to contingent factors external to divinity (Oppy 1995, 24, 219–223; Cargile 1975, 69; Downey 1986, 49).

Nonetheless, Oppy is perceptive to notice that Leibniz's version of the ontological argument was at least strong enough to inspire a version of the argument from Godel. His Axiom 3 and Theorem 1 (and its corollary) in the following rendition of his argument by C. Anthony Anderson are tantamount to the claim that a necessarily existent God is possible, a possibility that many (Oppy hyperbolizes when he says "all") atheists and agnostics would deny. Godel's argument goes something like this:

> Definition 1: x is Godlike iff x has as essential properties those and only those properties that are positive.
>
> Definition 2: A is an essence of x iff for every property B, x has B necessarily iff A entails B.
>
> Definition 3: x necessarily exists iff every essence of x is necessarily exemplified.
>
> Axiom 1: If a property is positive, then its negation is not positive.
>
> Axiom 2: Any property entailed by (i.e., strictly implied by) a positive property is positive.
>
> Axiom 3: The property of being Godlike is positive.
>
> Axiom 4: If a property is positive, then it is necessarily positive.
>
> Axiom 5: Necessary existence is positive.
>
> Theorem 1: If a property is positive, then it is consistent (i.e., possibly exemplified).
>
> Corollary 1: The property of being Godlike is consistent.
>
> Theorem 2: If something is Godlike, then the property of being Godlike is an essence of that thing.
>
> Theorem 3: Necessarily, the property of being Godlike is exemplified (Anderson 1990; Godel 1995; Oppy 1995, 224–225).

Of course there are questions concerning the undefined terms in this argument and concerning the truth of the axioms. I have cited Godel's version of the argument for one simple reason: to highlight the Leibnizian concern that defenders of the argument need not, as did Descartes, ignore the question of whether God's existence is possible.

In many respects Spinoza's use of the ontological argument in his *Ethics* is like Descartes', but Spinoza explicitly identified God as necessary in every respect, not merely in terms of necessary existence. This identification may very well be implicit in Descartes and other classical theists.

Spinoza's view led, as is well known, to a deterministic pantheism. We will see that if God's existence (i.e., the fact *that* God exists) as well as God's actuality (i.e., *how* God exists) are strictly necessary, then all things must be necessary, in which case not only is the meaning of the contrasting term "contingent" lost, but the distinctive meaning of "necessary" itself.

Spinoza's mistake in overextending the intellectual work done by the concept of necessity, however, is instructive in that he alerts us to a feature of the argument as it is used not only by pantheists, like Spinoza himself, but also by classical theists: even if divine existence can be inferred from an abstract concept, divine actuality cannot be so inferred – ". . . the necessary in God must be but an abstraction from [God's] total reality" (Hartshorne 1965, 108–109, 173–175; Plantinga 1965, 50–53). The task would be to indicate how God could be world-inclusive without falling into Spinoza's necessitarian pantheism; St. Paul may nonetheless be correct that we all live and move and have our being in God.

Of course many other figures would have to be mentioned, and much else would have to be said concerning the figures who have been mentioned, in order to provide anything like an adequate history of the ontological argument. But almost enough has been said thus far to paint the background against which the six contemporary authors who are the subjects of the present book will appear. Even a truncated history like the one offered here, however, needs to mention at least three other thinkers who operate in a major way in contemporary debates regarding the ontological argument. These are Gaunilo, Kant, and Hegel. These three historical figures are so central to contemporary debates that they will be discussed in the five chapters of the book devoted to contemporary appraisals of the ontological argument.

Hume and Theistic Metaphysics

One other historical figure will be treated here. Hume, along with Kant, is often thought to have driven the last nails needed in the ontological argument's coffin. But the alleged death of the ontological argument (like that of Mark Twain while he was still quite alive) is grossly exaggerated. As far as I can tell, it is not even sick. Hume may have thought that he killed the ontological argument, but he did not, like Schopenhauer, think that it was a charming joke. Hume took the argument quite seriously (Hartshorne 1965, 5, 125; Plantinga 1965, 65–67).

Consider the remarkable concession Hume seems to have made in his *Dialogues Concerning Natural Religion* (especially Part IX) to the effect that if the ontological argument happened to be sound, then we could dispose of the antitheistic argument based on the obvious evils in the world. This argument is often stated in a priori terms: if God has the classical theistic attribute of omnipotence, then the presence of evil in the world would disconfirm the existence of such a God in that an omnipotent God could eliminate evil. Hume realizes that a successful (and equally a priori) argument in favor of God's existence would bring down the argument from evil; the divine attributes would then have to be rethought. In short, if one *assumes* that God has a monopoly of power, then the presence of evil in the world disconfirms the existence of such a being. But is this assumption warranted? (Hartshorne 1965, 201; 2000, 417–418).

Indeed, the greatest conceivable being would have whatever properties it is better to have than not to have, but is monopoly of power and freedom such a property? Anselm's formula regarding "that than which no greater can be conceived" is (unwittingly) liberating in that it does not automatically lead, as Anselm thinks, to traditional theistic attributes. It is to Hume's credit that he saw the crucial connection between the theodicy problem and the ontological argument.

Unfortunately, he also assumed that whatever could be conceived of as existing could also be conceived of as not existing. One of the purposes of the present book is to try to meet this challenge in that it is doubtful that we can consistently conceive of the nonexistence of a perfect being. As Hartshorne puts the debate:

Anselm showed that Greatness is inconceivable except as necessarily existing; from which it was a corollary that to deny the conceivability of "necessarily existent" is to affirm "God is inconceivable". Hence the universal contingency of existence, affirmed by Hume as beyond all exception, is the downright denial even of the thinkability of deity. The stark contradiction between such absolute empiricism and theism does not necessarily refute theism; perhaps it rather refutes absolute empiricism! Moreover, the unqualified validity of empiricism cannot itself be an empirical truth. So Hume is simply appealing to his own a priori, against the religious a priori. (Hartshorne 1965, 206; 1984a, 213–217)

It should not be assumed that Hume's criticisms have a determinative effect on Oppy, the greatest contemporary critic of the ontological argument. Oppy thinks that Philo's speeches in the *Dialogues* (which presumably come closest to Hume's own view) do not represent Hume at his best. Oppy thinks that even if one can conceive of God as nonexistent, this does not show (as Hume thinks) that God's existence could not be demonstrated when God *is* distinctly conceived as that than which no greater can be conceived (Oppy 1995, 26–29; cf. Hartshorne 1923, 263–264; 1962, 108).

Further, Oppy objects to Jonathan Barnes' effort in the following Hume-like argument:

1. Nothing is demonstrable a priori unless the contrary implies a contradiction (premise).
2. Nothing that is distinctly conceivable entails a contradiction (premise).
3. Whatever we conceive as existent, we can also conceive as non-existent (premise).
4. Therefore, there is no being whose nonexistence implies a contradiction (from 2, 3).
5. Therefore, there is no being whose nonexistence is demonstrable a priori (from 1, 4) (Barnes 1972).

Oppy wonders whether it is really possible to make sense of the concept of necessary existence. Here, however, his primary concern is to allege that this Humean argument is simply question begging. This is because it conflates inconceivability, which is a psychological notion, and self-contradiction, which is a logical notion. By mixing psychological and logical considerations, Hume has made it too easy, on Oppy's view, to refute the ontological argument, which is claimed by its defenders to be logical. In addition, Oppy thinks that Hume contradicts himself when he says that whatever we conceive, we conceive as existent. If this is true, then we cannot *consistently* conceive of anything as nonexistent, as Hume alleges (Oppy 1995, 225–228).

Craig Harrison is more typical of opponents of the ontological argument, who generally take Hume to be one of their patron saints. Harrison objects to the fact that the ontological argument, which is supposedly a logical argument, requires premises that are nonlogical (and perhaps psychological, as Oppy alleges). This serves to weaken whatever force the argument would have had. As a result, Harrison defends Hume's premise that no proposition asserting the existence of an individual is universally (or necessarily) valid. That is, necessary existence cannot be demonstrated from logical principles alone without the aid of tendentious definitions. Harrison and Hume are like Oppy, however, in thinking that the ontological argument fails in philosophically interesting ways (Harrison 1970).

One of the features of the ontological argument that continues to make it interesting is that, even if Hume is correct that one cannot prove

the existence of something a priori unless the contrary implies a contradiction, he has still not thereby disproved the argument. This is because,
according to defenders of the argument, the denial of God's necessary
existence *does* imply a contradiction. Thus Hume's criticisms do not in
themselves destroy the modalized version of the argument (Purtill 1966,
401–402).

In addition to his influential comments that relate to the ontological
argument, Hume's philosophy is especially important because his own
implicit metaphysical stance is a major impetus behind contemporary
attacks on theistic metaphysics in general. Let us start with the understanding of a metaphysical doctrine in terms of a modal statement about
existence: saying what could, could not, or must exist. In other words,
statements in metaphysics are modal statements about what could, could
not, or could not fail to exist. Assuming this understanding of metaphysics, Hume is a metaphysician in at least three ways.

First, Hume holds in *A Treatise of Human Nature* (Book 1, Part 3, Section 6; also Part 1, Sections 1, 3) that nothing that is distinguishable from
something else could be inseparable from the other thing. That is, to be
distinct *means* to be separable, such that Hume is not stating a mere fact,
rather he is stating what is the case necessarily. Mutual independence is,
for Hume, a basic metaphysical principle regarding all things. However,
in a theistic metaphysics that involves a neoclassical defense of the ontological argument, not only is Hume's view here quite far from self-evident,
it is impossible (Hartshorne 1983, 136–137).

Second, Hume holds (Book 2, Part 3, Section 1) that strict determinism is logically possible. In fact, he asserts that determinism is true of
all existents. Hume is no doubt correct that the world is in some sense
orderly in that a *completely* unorderly world is a contradiction in terms, a
metaphysical impossibility. This is because merely to identify "the world"
is to presuppose *some* orderly state of affairs. But we should also ask the
opposite question: does *complete* order or *absolute* regularity or *strict* determinism make any more sense than complete disorder? Strict determinism
is not, it should be noted, an item that we experience, nor is it established
by observation. A safer position suggests that the order among existents
is neither absolute nor completely nonexistent (Hartshorne 1983, 137).

It will serve us well to pause at this point in the examination of the
relationship between Hume and theistic metaphysics. There is a discern-
able tendency that analytic philosophers exhibit, including those like
Bertrand Russell and others who have criticized theistic metaphysics, in
general, and the ontological argument, in particular. (Actually, at one

stage in his career Russell thought that the ontological argument was not only valid, but sound; later he thought in a Humean way that the argument was fallacious, even though even at this stage he admitted that it was not obvious which fallacy was committed – see Oppy 1995, 6–7.) And this tendency is one that has its origin in Hume, as Hartshorne rightly emphasizes. He asks the following concerning Hume:

> Is it not amazing that he should have maintained that although there is no logical connection whatever between events, there is nevertheless in fact not only a causal order in their occurrence, but an absolute, perfect, unqualified order? ... Hume thus combines two absolutes: absolute disconnectedness and absolute order. Observation cannot establish such absolutes, which must stand or fall as logical analysis supports or refutes them. They must be modal or else useless. (Hartshorne 1983, 137)

That is, Hume cannot be speaking as an empiricist when he establishes his metaphysics of the complete independence of each event from others. Rather, he is speaking of universal categories: the very idea of the *distinguishable* entails the idea of the *separable*. Likewise, we cannot empirically observe that the future is already determined. Determinism, like the idea that has held sway among many analytic philosophers that all facts are timeless, involves a metaphysical claim. Experience indicates to us that time is cumulative, such that later events are not mutually separable from their predecessors: the present is internally related to the past, but it is externally related to the future (Hartshorne 1983, 138–140).

Further, experience indicates to us that the future, unlike the past, is at least partially indeterminate or unsettled. It may very well be the case that later events implicate their predecessors, but they implicate what will happen in the future only in terms of possibility or probability:

> This is what a reasonable indeterminism holds; not that some concrete events "have no causes," but that the *exact* nature of ensuing events is left unspecified by the totality of their causal conditions. Something is left for the momentary self-determination of events. (Hartshorne 1983, 141–142)

To take a simple example, a calf may or may not become an adult cow, depending on whether or not the farmer decides that he likes the price being paid at present for veal, but every adult cow has been a calf.

The above two metaphysical principles found in Hume's *A Treatise of Human Nature* are at odds with the neoclassical theism that will be defended here. The third principle that should be mentioned fares no better. It is found in the *Dialogues Concerning Natural Religion* (again, Part IX) and it even more forcefully intersects theism, in general, and a defense of the ontological argument, in particular. Hume is quite forthright in claiming that nothing can exist by necessity. It is not merely that nothing does exist by necessity, but that nothing *could* exist by necessity. Further, he thinks that the idea that existence could follow from a mere concept, property, or logical possibility is itself an impossibility. Given these claims (reiterated in different language by Oppy, despite his criticisms of Hume in other respects), it is not surprising that Hume rejects the ontological argument.

There is no escaping the modal character of Hume's view: a necessary existent *could not be*; and it is *impossible* that existence follow from a concept, property, or logical possibility. Even if Hume had said that in fact nothing exists by necessity, he would be implying, at the very least, that it is *possible* that all things could be contingent in their modes of existence. In a comment that could apply to Oppy as well as to Hume, Hartshorne urges the following:

Modal status is itself always necessary. That facts of the ordinary kind are contingent is not itself contingent; they could not be necessary (or impossible). Thus to deny a modal statement is to make one. It is therefore mere begging of the question to say that while Anselm needs to prove his contention in his ontological argument, Hume and others do not. (Hartshorne 1983, 142–143)

There are statements regarding existence whose negation it is impossible to conceive, contra Hume. For example, there is the statement that "Something exists." There seems to be no experienceable alternative to the existence of *something* in that the very experience of the alternative would exist. We can easily imagine the nonexistence of spotted owls in North America, but can we easily, if at all, imagine the nonexistence of a perfect being? To say that the necessary existence of God is made intelligible by the ontological argument is *not* to say, as the argument's detractors often allege, that one is thereby moving from an abstract concept to concrete reality. This is because, as a result of a neoclassical use of the ontological argument, there must be concrete instances of divine existence from moment to moment, but *which* instances can only be contingent. Hume (unwittingly) aids the case for neoclassical theism by holding that an individual thing or substance is not the most concrete or most actual level of existence if an individual thing or substance is itself an abstraction away from momentary states or events. As a result, the divine individual is an abstraction when contrasted to *how* the divine individual exists from moment to moment (Hartshorne 1983, 144–145). Analogously, to say *that* I exist is quite abstract; to say that I exist as a 52-year-old human being is more concrete, although still quite abstract; to say that I am a 52-year-old human being who has not shaved today because I am out of razors is more concrete still; and so on.

As with "something," there must be an instance of "that than which no greater can be conceived." At the very least, the ontological argument is negatively conclusive against the casual dismissal of theism: even if we cannot conceive of God with optimal clarity and distinctness (a point that Hartshorne is willing to concede), we also cannot conceive of God or the perfect being as nonexistent. In any event, a "concept claiming necessity has to be dealt with modally, by logical analysis, not by observation" (Hartshorne 1983, 146). That is, truths regarding necessary existence are arrived at through the discovery of consistent meanings, not by empirical facts or observations, as the legacy of Hume has, by way of contrast, implied. The following summary of the impact of Hume's view on those who would continue to develop theistic metaphysics is quite helpful:

> Humeanism is dogmatically metaphysical in its basic notions of the symmetrical, logical independence of events, the symmetrical causal inferrability of later from earlier and vice versa, and the complete symmetrical independence of thought from reality; hence the universal contingency of all types of existential judgments. There are excellent reasons for regarding events as asymmetrically dependent, causal order as only relatively deterministic, and thought as in its most abstract aspects necessarily exemplified in existence. (Hartshorne 1983, 147)

Ultimately, Hume's position is problematic because it rests on several a priori axioms. They are problematic not because they are a priori, but because they lead to conclusions that contradict each other. For example, his belief that the distinguishable is always separable radically disconnects reality, whereas his defense of a strict determinism radically connects it. In effect, a supposedly pure empiricism like Hume's is insufficient. This insufficiency, I will argue, is also common in certain contemporary critics of the ontological argument.

As mentioned earlier, this truncated history will be supplemented later in the book with treatments of three other key historical figures: Gaunilo (Chapter 5), Kant (Chapter 5), and Hegel (Chapter 3). So those scholars who are especially fond of Gaunilo's or Kant's criticisms of the argument, or of Hegel's expansive use of it, will have to be patient.

2

Poetry versus the Ontological Argument

Richard Rorty's Challenge

Daniel Dennett asks whether the stirrings of Richard Rorty's later ideas can be seen in between the lines of his "early" papers in analytic philosophy of mind. The differences between the two Rortys are encapsulated in the two different definitions found in Dennett's joke dictionary of philosophers' names. The first is that a "rort" is "an incorrigible report, hence rorty, incorrigible." The second, by way of contrast, is the adjective "a rortiori," which refers to something that is "true for even more fashionable continental reasons." Dennett rightly wonders about how Rorty went from being an author who wrote for a small coterie of analytic philosophers of mind in the early 1970s to being what Harold Bloom, say, sees as an international man of letters, indeed as the most interesting philosopher in the world! (Dennett 2000; Malachowski 2003).

One of my purposes is to push back Dennett's concerns even further, to the early 1960s, when Rorty was very much interested in process philosophy and neoclassical theism, as is evident from his publications from this period (Rorty 1963a; 1963b; 1963c; 1963d). We can analogously ask whether the stirrings of Rorty's later ideas can be seen in between the lines of his *really* early papers, which deal with Alfred North Whitehead and Charles Hartshorne. This question is, at the very least, of historical significance, but Rorty's return to his critique of process thought and neoclassical theism in a 1995 response to an article by Hartshorne indicates that an understanding of the conceptual relationship between Rorty and Hartshorne is crucial for an understanding of each thinker individually (Hartshorne 1995; Rorty 1995). Indeed, a study of the conceptual relationship between Rorty and Hartshorne is instructive regarding the problems involved in getting a fair hearing for contemporary metaphysics and the ontological argument in that, as Rorty sees things, poetry (in the wide sense of the term he uses) trumps metaphysics.

Before examining the conceptual relationship between these two thinkers, however, the personal connection between them should not escape our notice. Rorty balances his "pull no punches" approach to Hartshorne's thought, including Hartshorne's treatment of the ontological argument, with the acknowledgment that as a 19-year-old student at the University of Chicago he was initially drawn to a career in philosophy due to Hartshorne as a teacher and as a person, and he remained as a philosophy major, despite the temptation to leave, due to Hartshorne's influence. Regarding Hartshorne as a person, it was his intellectual passion and his generosity of spirit that were especially noteworthy, according to Rorty. Further, Rorty wrote his M.A. thesis under Hartshorne on the topic of Whitehead's creativity as "the category of the ultimate." Interestingly, Rorty's characteristic emphasis on the contingent as opposed to the necessary is evident even at this early stage of his career in his claim that Whitehead's eternal objects are out of tune with the rest of Whitehead. This emphasis on the contingent, found very early in Rorty's career, portends his eventual rejection of the modal version of the ontological argument, which tries to establish God's existence as *necessary*. Despite his alleged generosity of spirit, Hartshorne notes only that Rorty was a former student who became famous (Rorty 1995, 29, 36; 1979, xiii; Hartshorne 1990, 233).

It should be emphasized at the outset that this chapter deals more generally with the possibility of metaphysics than do the other chapters, which deal more explicitly with the particular metaphysical project found in the ontological argument.

Some Important Concessions

Rorty's debt to Hartshorne, however, is not solely that of a student who continues to be appreciative of the fact that his former teacher helped him to find the right career. I have already mentioned Rorty's dissatisfaction with Whitehead's "Platonic" eternal objects, a dissatisfaction that was no doubt encouraged by Hartshorne's own criticism of this aspect of Whitehead's philosophy. As is well known, Hartshorne defends not eternal objects, but rather a theory of emergent universals. In this regard, Hartshorne is less of a Platonist than Whitehead, despite Plato's anticipation of the ontological argument (Ford 1973; Dombrowski 1991, 465–487, 703–704; 2005).

There are at least three other areas where Rorty acknowledges a conceptual debt to Hartshorne and concedes Hartshorne's achievements. All of these are relevant to an understanding and criticism of the ontological argument. First, and most important, is that Rorty, a lifelong and (by his own admission, sardonic) atheist, says that "*if* I could ever get myself to believe in God, it would certainly be a finite God of the sort described by Mill, James, Whitehead, and Hartshorne" (Rorty 1995, 29; 1999, 163). (Rorty mistakenly identifies Hartshorne's God as finite, whereas Hartshorne believes in the more complex view that God is infinite or everlasting or necessary in existence and finite in actuality – i.e., in the mode of divine existence in real relation with finite creatures.) Of course Rorty does not believe that there really is a divine fellow sufferer who understands. Indeed, he thinks he "can carry on perfectly well" without a God. But the fellow sufferer who understands is the sort of being *who would be* a God if such a being were to exist (Rorty 1995, 34).

Despite the ironic positivist sound to Rorty's view here (ironic because of Rorty's accusation that the positivists were just one more species of foundationalists and defenders of just one more version of the correspondence theory of truth), his 1995 concession to Hartshorne is in evidence in his early writings as well. That is, if we ask *why* Rorty thinks that the process or neoclassical God is superior to that of classical theists, we can find an answer in his early essays.

Consider his 1963 essay "Matter and Event," where his criticisms of Aristotle are precisely those offered by Whitehead and Hartshorne. On Rorty's reading, Aristotle was opposed both to materialist (atomist) reductions of form to matter (see *De Generatione et Corruptione* Book I, Chapter 2) as well as to Platonic reductions of matter to form (see *Metaphysics* Book I, Chapter 6). Reality is unavoidably complex in the Aristotelian "hylomorphic analysis of substance." Rorty also seems to agree with Whitehead and Hartshorne with the claim that "Aristotle betrayed his own better insights when, in *Metaphysics* XII, he made room for the Unmoved Mover – the perfect case of a vacuous actuality" (Rorty 1963a, 507). This abandonment of a unity that is internally complex has had a disastrous effect on the history of philosophic thought about God, including the God whose necessary existence is urged in the ontological argument, according to the process view that Rorty endorses.

Here Rorty relies on John Herman Randall regarding what Aristotle *should have* said in order to maintain hylomorphism at the cosmological level, a cosmic hylomorphism that is exemplified most prominently in contemporary philosophy by Hartshorne's frequent defense of the ancient Greek (especially Plato's) concept of the World Soul: God is the soul for the body of the whole world. Does God exist totally apart from the world of moving things? Hartshorne's own response, and the response that Randall/Rorty think that Aristotle should have made in order to remain consistent to his hylomorphism, is: no. To be God is to be necessarily existent, but it is also to be the living form of the world's matter, "the *energeia* and *entelecheia* of its *dynameis*" (Randall 1960, 143–144; also Rorty 1963a, 504, 507). God would be nothing if God were not the essential factor *of the world*, specifically the harmony of the natural ends of particular things in the world. Aristotle himself flirts with cosmic hylomorphism, even if he does not consistently defend it (*Metaphysics* Book XII, Chapter 10, especially 1075a).

So also, on a consistent version of cosmic hylomorphism that avoids Rorty's aversion to both free-floating eternal objects and disembodied divine agency, God would be immanent in the world as its intelligible order even if God would also *in a sense* transcend the world as its ideal end. God as an Unmoved Mover (or the gods as unmoved movers) ruins this internal-external balance, however (Randall 1960, 143–144; Rorty 1963a, 502).

Aristotle's mistake, on Rorty's reading, a mistake remedied in Hartshorne's World Soul-oriented theism, was to make an

... illicit transition from the doctrine of form-as-the-actuality-of-the-matter to the notion of form-as-the-actuality-of-the-composite-substance. This transition evolved into the notion of form-in-isolation contributing something called "actuality" to the composite substance, whereas matter-in-isolation contributed the element of "potentiality." (Rorty 1963a, 509–510)

This transition kept alive the worst aspects of "Platonism," on Rorty's view, a Platonism that Rorty has assailed throughout his career, especially in his magnum opus, *Philosophy and the Mirror of Nature* (Dombrowski 1988a). Aristotle's Unmoved Mover, with its associated "Platonic" escape from matter, is also, on Rorty's interpretation, an escape from decision making altogether. Rorty's implied stance, by contrast, is that the greatest conceivable being, if such existed, would be the one who makes the most important and far-reaching decisions, as is the case in Hartshorne's theism, rather than a being who escapes from decision making altogether (Rorty 1963a, 512; Hartshorne 1936).

Rorty not only favors process or neoclassical theism to the classical theism often found in the Abrahamic religions (with Aristotle's Unmoved Mover being the main predecessor to classical theism), he also seems to favor Hartshorne's version of neoclassical theism to Whitehead's because the latter's Primordial Nature of God, which contemplates the "Platonic" eternal objects, is ironically too close to Aristotle's Unmoved Mover. There are notorious passages in Whitehead where God is seen as a non-temporal actuality, rather than as an everlasting temporal series of divine occasions, as in Hartshorne's concept of the greatest conceivable being-in-becoming (Rorty 1963a, 519).

Despite Rorty's thorough knowledge of process thought, he is not always an accurate guide in what he says about Hartshorne. For example, he compares the delight the neoclassical God takes in creation to fans of the avant garde who go to galleries to be astonished, rather than to have any particular expectation fulfilled (Rorty 1999, 28). But this trivializes divine care for the world in light of the immense suffering that human beings have experienced and continue to experience. God cares for creation not the way trendy arts enthusiasts "care for" the latest hip painter, but rather in a way appropriate to a perfect, omnibenevolent being who is moved in relation to creaturely suffering. Further, there are metaphysical reasons why a relational God cannot remain unmoved by the creatures' suffering.

The undeniable fact of suffering is one of the reasons why Hartshorne rejects belief in divine omnipotence. This suffering is largely due, on Hartshorne's view, to the presence of widespread contingency in the world and to the inadvertent clash of conflicting freedoms. Rorty gives approval to the pervasiveness of contingency in Hartshorne's philosophy (despite the latter's defense of the ontological argument, with its conclusion dealing with God's necessary existence), wherein there is a coincidence of real and logical possibility. "Possible worlds" are real possibilities, not merely logical ones. Possibilities that are "merely logical," on Hartshorne's view, refer either to what were real possibilities in the remote past or to what will be – or could be – real possibilities in the remote future. Although it is convenient to speak of merely logical possibilities, this is ultimately an inaccurate way of describing them. Although Rorty is skeptical regarding whether we could ever have such perfect command of our ideas that we could see the logical absurdity in any description that is really impossible, he agrees with Hartshorne that: "There can be no exact or ultimate 'why' for the contingent. The contingent is the arbitrary, the not strictly deducible" (Hartshorne 1963a, 599; also Rorty 1963c, 606). The idea that there are timeless truths (the idea most detested by Rorty) has done the greatest amount of harm, Hartshorne thinks, in religion. Once again, this claim is made despite his defense of the ontological argument. Indeed, Hartshorne thinks that the idea that there are time-independent truths is "downright vicious" because it encourages us to "retreat from our responsibilities by indulging in superstitious prophecies" (Hartshorne 1963a, 605). It is presumably this sort of strong language that makes Hartshorne's theism so appealing to Rorty.

However, Rorty rejects theism in part because the question regarding the existence of God is intimately connected to the question regarding the correspondence theory of truth: if there is an omniscient point of view held by the greatest conceivable being (however omniscience is defined) then there is the possibility that someone – either God (really) or us (vicariously) – might "get things right."

Second, Rorty praises Whitehead's and Hartshorne's relationalism, which Hartshorne himself emphasizes in a phrase that is the title of one of his books: reality as *social* process. In fact, Rorty thinks that historians of philosophy will eventually see the twentieth century as a period where a Leibnizian "panrelationalism" was developed under several different rubrics. The key idea is that each monad (however "monad" is defined) is related to all the other monads seen from a certain perspective.

In nonprocess language, the way to put it would be in terms of each substance involving relations to all the other substances. Whitehead's way of putting the point is to say that every actual occasion is constituted by relations to all other actual occasions. Hartshorne's even more convincing way to state the matter is to say that an actual occasion or an event is internally related to its past, but externally related to "its" future. Each actual occasion's decision regarding the impact from its past and from God is what distinguishes it as the occasion it is.

Once again, the process critique of Aristotle (specifically, the critique of Aristotle's notion of substance) is praised by Rorty even if, on Hartshorne's view, Rorty does not fully appreciate the significance of the "event standpoint." Rorty allies process relationalism with Peirce's and Russell's and Wittgenstein's separate attempts to formulate a nonsubject/predicate logic and, surprisingly, with Derrida's criticism of logocentrism and view (shared with Quine) of words as nodes in a flexible web of relationships with other words (Rorty 1999, 69–70; 1967, 125–133; Hartshorne 1983, 168).

And third, in addition to supporting Hartshorne's version of neoclassical theism and his relationalism, Rorty, in his early essays at least, seems to approve of the efforts of process thinkers, including Hartshorne, in dealing with "the central task of contemporary philosophy." This task, as Rorty saw things in 1963, was to reconcile the fact that all knowledge is

perspectival with "the fact that knowledge is about objects distinct from
and independent of the experiencing subject." That is, the central task
of contemporary philosophy, a task willingly taken up by Whitehead and
Hartshorne, is to reconcile perspectivalism with realism. What the early
Rorty seems to find especially helpful in process thought's "reformed
subjectivist principle" is the idea that not only the subjects of knowledge,
but also the objects known, can only be described in "token-reflexive
terms." By token-reflexive terms Rorty means those terms that make sentences capable of different truth values depending on the circumstances
in which the sentences are made (Rorty 1963d, 153–154). However, the
need for token-reflexive terms does not militate against a defense of the
ontological argument.

Because of the need for token-reflexive terms like "this," "there,"
"now," "then," and so on, "it is logically impossible," Rorty thinks, in
agreement with process thinkers, "that there should be a description of
reality which is not a description from a perspective which is one among
alternative perspectives." But this does not necessarily constitute a sur-
render to idealism. Realism is compatible with the view that "there can
be no such thing as 'the complete description of reality.'" The contingency of statements about temporal locations seems to be part of the
very fabric not only of discourse, but of *reality itself.* One of the reasons
why a complete description of reality is not possible is that if experience
is synonymous with *present* experienced togetherness, then the concrete
entities that make up the world are unrepeatable, in contrast to what
Whitehead saw as the repeatability of the eternal objects (or to what
Hartshorne calls universals).

Or at least Rorty so thought in 1963 in an essay that he still viewed
(surprisingly, given his later abandonment of realism) as largely correct
as late as 1995 (Rorty 1995, 211; 1963d). Even in the early 1960s, however, Rorty disagreed with certain aspects of process thought in addition
to Hartshorne's defense of the ontological argument, a defense that had
reached its peak at this time. Most notably he disagreed with the effort to
explicate the problematic features of knowing by reference to unproblematic features of *feeling.* Rorty, by contrast, explicated problematic features of knowing by reference to unproblematic features of *talking.* That
is, on Rorty's view, there is something suspicious about a process view of
intentionality that is built on the presence of one actuality in another,
say through memory or perception or prehension. But, at least at this
early stage in his career, Rorty was not opposed to *some* version of intentionality when seen as "the reference of every conscious judgment to an

entity capable of existing independently of that judgment" (Rorty 1963d, 152–155; also Hartshorne 1955).

It is plausible to read the really early Rorty as saying that the realism of Whitehead and Hartshorne is superior to Aristotle's realism because Whitehead and Hartshorne consistently take time seriously (i.e., they acknowledge the need for token-reflexive terms). Further, process thinkers are realists not only with respect to ordinary things (like Aristotle's primary substances), but also with respect to actual occasions. This inclusion of time (specifically, for Rorty, of token-reflexive terms) and of actual occasions and an event ontology, rather than substances, "permits one to save realism," according to Rorty, as well as to improve on Strawson's commonsense Aristotelianism (Rorty 1963a, 523; 1998, 250; Chappell 1963). Finally, as is well known, this inclusion has a major impact on one's concept of God.

Rejection of Metaphysics

Despite these three major concessions to Hartshorne, the amount of rapprochement between Rorty and Hartshorne is rather restricted. To put the point simply: Rorty is opposed to metaphysics and the ontological argument and Hartshorne is primarily a metaphysician and a defender of the ontological argument. But the subtleties of each thinker's position are worthy of exploration because they indicate why the contemporary controversy over metaphysics is quite different from the earlier one in the twentieth century that involved the positivists.

Opposition to Demonstration

Rorty tells us quite explicitly that when he read one of Hartshorne's greatest books, and perhaps the most tightly written, *The Divine Relativity*, he was "put off by all the attempts at demonstration, all the stuff about modality, all the talk of necessary metaphysical truth." Rorty's complaint is that Hartshorne tries to mix oil and water, in effect binding the spirit of Christ to the fetters of Euclid, to use Rorty's language (Rorty 1995, 29–30; Hartshorne 1948).

Despite my general defense of Hartshorne's views, and my general negativity regarding Rorty's, I must admit that Rorty is on to something here. He may very well be correct that the key tension in Hartshorne's thought that still needs careful explication is the relationship between the data of concrete religious experience and the rationalist formalism and argumentation found throughout his writings, the latter of which is operative in the defense of the ontological argument. I would like to make it clear that I do not share Rorty's assessment that Hartshorne leans too far in the direction of rationalistic metaphysics, but his locating of the crucial tension in Hartshorne is no small achievement.

Awareness of Mortality

Rorty thinks that we are "better off without metaphysics" and presumably better off without the ontological argument. He describes the desire to do metaphysics in Heideggerian terms: awareness of our mortality leads us to want realities that are *meta ta physica*, beyond the physical ones. Whether this description fits Hartshorne, as Rorty thinks it does, is open to question when Hartshorne's repeated denial of subjective immortality is considered, as well as his repeated denial that God (the World Soul) completely transcends the physical (Dombrowski 2004, Ch. 10). Surely the desire to do metaphysics is not essentially connected to the desire to live on after our bodies die. But let us agree momentarily with Rorty so as to understand his line of thought. The idea seems to be that if the desire to do metaphysics is brought about by a misguided hope that we might escape death, then a solid dose of Wittgensteinian philosophical therapy will cure us of this desire (Rorty 1995, 31–34).

In fairness to Rorty it should be noted that the escape from death that he is criticizing might be metaphorical rather than literal. Hartshorne obviously rejects any sort of literal subjective immortality, as Rorty no doubt is aware, but his idea that we contribute our experiences to an everlasting God who exists necessarily might be, from Rorty's point of view, a vicarious escape from matter.

Contra Metaphysical Indeterminism

The hope Rorty has is that this therapy will result in metaphysical "problems" being dissolved, including the problem of God. When they are dissolved, both religion and science will, in turn, yield their places to poetry, to Wordsworth. But more later on religion, science, and Wordsworth. At this point in my treatment of the relationship between Rorty and Hartshorne we can see that much is at stake in Rorty's criticism of metaphysics: the demise of religion *and* science and the triumphal rise of Wordsworth and poetry, in general. Rorty sums up his critique of metaphysics (with special attention paid to the metaphysical dispute between freedom and determinism) in the following way:

... whereas Hartshorne thinks it important to defend indeterminism as a metaphysical truth, I think that reassurance on this metaphysical point has nothing to contribute to the development of an ever freer, more creative, more interesting culture. I agree with Hume and Kant that we are going to carry on as if we were free, regardless of whether physics is currently siding with the determinists or the indeterminists. I do not think it matters whether we accept "the essentially creative aspect of becoming" as long as we keep trying to create ever more open space for the play of the human imagination. I see cultural politics, rather than metaphysics, as the context in which to place everything else. (Rorty 1995, 35)

On Rorty's reading, metaphysics conceived in the Hartshornian sense consists of "the urge to find necessary truths and real modalities" – in other words, "the urge for transcendentality" – and is thus a result of the epistemological quest for certainty. But epistemological certainty is not attainable, according to Rorty and process thinkers alike (as discussed earlier, regarding Rorty's treatment of token-reflexive terms in process thought). Therefore, metaphysical truth is opposed to process philosophy itself, he thinks (Rorty 1995, 36).

The Denial of Relativism
Rorty is well aware of how radical his critique is. His antimetaphysical stance is nothing short of an attempt to critique (or better, to reject) a philosophical tradition that goes back to Plato, including Plato's anticipation of the ontological argument. By dissolving metaphysical problems through Wittgensteinian therapy applied to thinkers like Hartshorne, Rorty knows that he will be accused of being a reductionist and a relativist. He responds to these accusations by repudiating almost the entire philosophical lexicon inherited from Plato: the distinctions between finding and making, discovery and invention, objectivity and subjectivity, absolute and relative, and, of particular importance here, the distinction between the necessary and the contingent. He agrees with Heidegger that metaphysics *is* Platonism. According to Rorty, this is precisely why Whitehead thought that the safest possible characterization of Western philosophy was that it was a series of footnotes to Plato. By rejecting metaphysics and the Platonic tradition that has so profoundly affected Whitehead and Hartshorne, Rorty hopes to start over (Rorty 1999, xviii).

Another distinction that Rorty rejects is that between theism and atheism. Thus, he has recently apologized for previously characterizing himself as an atheist. That is, he does not want to be heard to say that atheism is true because it more accurately describes the way the world is than does theism. Rorty now prefers to characterize his view as beyond the theism-atheism debate. But he admits that he is "religiously unmusical," that he does not hear what St. Paul does when he says *fides ex auditu* (hearing is believing), meaning Rorty is tone deaf when it comes to religion. Hence it is clear that he is closer to atheism than he is to theism. And he is decidedly an atheist *if* what this means is to be anticlericalist and opposed to organized religion exercising political influence (Rorty 2005; also 2002; 2003).

We have seen Rorty's concession that the theistic metaphysics of process thinkers like Hartshorne is superior to alternative versions of theistic metaphysics. But this is a far cry from showing the superiority of theistic metaphysics to other ways of doing philosophy, he thinks. Consider Rorty's review of Victor Lowe's *Understanding Whitehead* from the early 1960s. He thinks that Lowe and Whitehead are to be praised for pointing out the "fallacy of the perfect dictionary," the belief that human beings have entertained all of the fundamental ideas regarding experience and that human language can adequately express these ideas. Scientists, at least, establish convincing criteria to determine what additions to make to this dictionary (Rorty later is more demure regarding science), but metaphysicians do not do so in any convincing way. Their best effort in this regard consists in saying that by reconceiving experience as part of a theistic metaphysics, we are able to appreciate for the first time aspects of experience that are always present, and hence are usually not the focus of attention. What is needed is a more careful comparison on the part of process thinkers of theistic metaphysics with the various antimetaphysical views defended in contemporary philosophy. Hartshorne is better than other theistic metaphysicians in this regard, Rorty thinks, but even Hartshorne engages nontheists "only generally and vaguely" (Rorty 1963b).

"Getting Things Right"

Process metaphysicians have successfully reached an accommodation with Darwin, Rorty thinks, but this accomplishment is not as significant as it seems initially. All they have done, on his interpretation, is to present in temporalized language the old Platonic distinctions, especially that between "the rational pursuit of the truth by the wise and the flux of passion characteristic of the many" (Rorty 1995, 200). Or again, despite the process criticisms of Aristotle already noted, process thinkers keep alive the Aristotelian notion of the identity of subject and object. And it is precisely this knowledge-as-identity thesis (like knows like) that preserves the correspondence theory of truth that the skeptic Rorty wishes to demolish (Rorty 2000, 219). (Of course to call Rorty a skeptic is to presuppose some of the old Platonic distinctions that Rorty thinks we should transcend.) Rorty's skepticism is not new. Even in the early 1960s, in some comments on a paper by Hartshorne, he indicated that the hope that we would one day *know* the laws of nature "seems irrelevant to our own situation," a stance that clearly paves the way for his later truth-as-coherence position that is at odds, it seems, with any defense of the ontological argument (Rorty 1963c, 606).

It is not insignificant, according to Rorty, that at the University of Chicago Hartshorne had formed something of an alliance with Rudolf Carnap. Both shared a taste for the formal and the necessary (although Carnap obviously did not extend this taste to include the necessary existence of God). Rorty did not and he does not share such a taste. Rather, he cheered the publication of Quine's famous "Two Dogmas" article; and he did the same regarding Wittgenstein's *Philosophical Investigations*, especially when Wittgenstein asked the question, "Why did we think that logic was something sublime?" Rorty is thus opposed to the formal and the necessary when they are used by empiricists like Carnap and especially when they are used by metaphysicians like Hartshorne in his defense of the ontological argument. That is, linguistic philosophy becomes more exciting when it turns away from Carnap-like formalism. Rorty's very first philosophical article was an attempt to ally Wittgenstein with another temporalistic critic of "Platonism": Peirce. But the hero here is the process Peirce of evolutionary love, in contrast to the formalistic Peirce of the logic of relatives. It makes sense that Rorty's temporalistic focus is very much compatible with, indeed it is indebted to, Hartshorne's temporalistic focus, but not with Hartshorne's formalism (Rorty 1961; 1995, 30).

Despite Rorty's belief that scientists can more fruitfully add to the aforementioned imagined perfect dictionary than can theistic metaphysicians, there is agreement between Rorty and Hartshorne that most religious believers and most scientists share a common faith in the ability of human beings to think in ways that correspond with reality, a faith that Rorty lacks. Rorty is willing to dispense with the "connaturality" of ourselves with the rest of reality in large part because he does not think that connaturality is required in order for us to find meaning in life. In fact, Rorty sees natural science as the Enlightenment version of religion. Both natural science and religion allege to put us in contact with ultimate reality:

By contrast, I tend to view natural science as in the business of controlling and predicting things, and as largely useless for philosophical purposes. Whereas Hartshorne views phenomena like quantum indeterminacy as a tip-off to metaphysical truth, I suspect that science will not converge to agreement with either panpsychists or materialists. (Rorty 1995, 32; 1979, 113–117; Hartshorne 1995, 24–25)

The Rortean Utopia looks not toward scientists or technicians, nor toward prophets or priests, but rather to poets "as the cutting edge of civilization." Rorty sums up his view of the alliance between science and religion in the following terms:

I think the problem with religious people and scientists is that they think it important not simply to create, but to get something right. I should like to free Whitehead's Category of the Ultimate not just from the theory of eternal objects [along with Hartshorne], but from the fetters of the correspondence theory of truth, and from the idea that we need a super-science called metaphysics [contra Hartshorne]. (Rorty 1995, 34)

Political Implications

The rejection of metaphysics and the ontological argument by Rorty, it should be added, has political implications. If there is no source of obligation other than the claims of "sentient beings" (a view that should not necessarily be seen as a concession on Rorty's part to animal rightists – Dombrowski 1983; 1988b), then responsibility to God or Truth or Reason should be replaced by our responsibility to each other. Theistic metaphysics is valuable, on this hypothesis, only in a utilitarian or pragmatic way when religious belief cultivates habits of action that further, or at least do not frustrate, the needs of other human beings. That is, theistic metaphysics can be valuable, but not because it "gets something right."

This utilitarian or pragmatic view of religion was Mill's view, as well as William James's, but it is obviously not Hartshorne's in any unqualified way. The Rortean strategy here is to privatize theistic metaphysics and to allow religious believers the freedom to practice their religion as long as they do not bring claims to knowledge of the divine will into the public arena. This privatization is problematic in relation to the ontological argument in that defenders of the argument claim that it is sound in a public way that can be understood by different rational agents. As Rorty sees things, however, this privatization is open not only to religious believers, but also to other "foundationalists" (Rorty's designation) who are empiricists, common sensists, and so forth. People have a right to faith in addition to a right to fall in love, he admits:

Pragmatist theists, however, do have to get along without personal immortality, providential intervention, the efficacy of sacraments, the Virgin Birth, the Risen Christ, the Covenant with Abraham, the authority of the Koran.... Or, if they want them, they will have to interpret them "symbolically".... Demythologizing amounts to saying that, whatever theism is good for, it is not a device for predicting or controlling our environment. (Rorty 1999, 156–157)

But even science, in predicting and controlling our environment, is like religion in being what it is due to the fact that human beings have the interests they do. But "scientific realism and religious fundamentalism are products of the same urge": specifically the out of control urge to get things right (Rorty 1999, 157).

This contrast between utilitarian or pragmatist philosophy of religion and fundamentalist religion is analogous, on Rorty's view, to the contrast between *faith*, on the one hand, and a more ambitious *belief in creeds or rational proofs* for the existence of God, such as the ontological argument, on the other. Faith, he thinks, as opposed to belief in creeds or arguments for the existence of God, is, for some unexplained reason, more likely to lead to love or some other socially beneficial emotion (Rorty 1999, 158, 166; MacIntyre and Ricoeur 1969). The religious faith that Rorty tolerates is one that is conducive to *our* doing vast good, rather than a whimsical hope that God will do so. We do not need to look beyond nature to the supernatural, on Rorty's view, nor should we do so.

Hartshorne's theistic metaphysics and his defense of the ontological argument, however, are no more types of supernaturalism than they are types of religiosity that encourage or require a belief in personal immortality, virgin birth, and so on, contra Rorty. Nor is it clear how Hartshorne's (fallibilist) arguments for the existence of God make him an ally of the fundamentalists. To be precise, Rorty is opposed not only to supernatural theism (as is Hartshorne, in that God is the soul that informs the body of the *natural* world: the World Soul), but to *any* theistic metaphysics. The closest he comes to religious belief or to something ultimate is in those rare moments when he is not content with utilitarianism, nor with pragmatic coping, but yearns for validity (soundness?) as well (Rorty 1999, 159–163).

It is instructive to try to get behind Rorty's meat-cleaver distinction between utilitarian (or pragmatic) philosophy of religion and fundamentalism, which he thinks roughly corresponds to the distinction between Protestantism and Catholicism, respectively, as if some Protestants were not fundamentalists and as if some Catholics were not familiar with symbolic or spiritual readings of scripture in the tradition of *lectio divina* (Rorty 1999, 158, 166). His underlying concern is that "fundamentalist" religion is a "conversation stopper" in a liberal society where people differ regarding what Rawls calls various comprehensive doctrines, sometimes differing uncompromisingly. But whereas Rawls leaves open the possibility that a theistic metaphysics could be true, and presumably that the ontological argument might be sound, and that citizens can believe in a theistic metaphysics as long as they do not violate the rights of others along the way, Rorty is convinced that such a metaphysics is a bogus hypothesis, hence it is best to have citizens privatize it. Rawls, once again by way of contrast with Rorty, notices that religious believers tend to worship in community, hence freedom of religion is not to be equated with Rortean privatization (Dombrowski 2001a).

It is unclear if Rorty is correct in equating his privatization of religion with one of Whitehead's definitions of religion in *Religion in the Making* in terms of what we *do* with our solitariness. Perhaps we will choose to identify with others in a faith (or creedal) community, hence escaping privatization. Or we might share our thoughts with others regarding arguments for the existence of God. Further, Rortean liberalism is different from Rawlsian liberalism to the extent that the latter, but not the former, *does* allow religion in the public square as long as the proviso is met that the parochial terms of one's religious belief are eventually translated into terms that any reasonable person could understand. Both Rawls and Rorty agree, however, that not much is to be gained, and much could be lost, if we debated the merits of theistic metaphysics or of the ontological argument *in politics*.

It should be emphasized in this regard that both Whitehead and Hartshorne were political liberals. Despite the subtle differences in their respective political stances, they were much closer to Rawls than to Rorty regarding the points just discussed, especially because of Rorty's rejection of the possibility that a theistic metaphysics could be true or that the ontological argument could be sound, and, in Hartshorne's case, because of a willingness to avoid parochial language and neologisms such that any reasonable person can understand what he is trying to get at in his theistic metaphysics and in his defense of the ontological argument (Rorty 1999, 168–174; Dombrowski 1997).

A Hartshornian Response

It must be admitted that any interpreter of Hartshorne is confronted with the tension in his thought between the experiential and the contingent and the formal and the necessary, as Rorty correctly notes.

The Experiential and the Contingent

To take just one example, consider what Hartshorne says about the role of religious experience in his view of God. In *Omnipotence and Other Theological Mistakes* (1984b) he pointed out the implausibility in every other area of life of a thoroughgoing egalitarianism with respect to degree of skill or insight. Some people play the piano better than others, construct houses better than others, shoot a jump shot better than others. Why not in religion, too? Some individuals seem to have clearer, deeper, and more authentic religious insights and experiences than others: Jesus, Moses, Mohammed, for starters, but also the Buddha, George Fox, Anselm, Lao Tse, Confucius, Zoroaster, Sankara, Teilhard de Chardin, Teresa of Avila, Mary Baker Eddy, Dietrich Bonhoeffer, Hildegard of Bingen, Black Elk, and Thomas Merton. The list could be extended quite a bit.

None of these "experts" in religious experience is infallible, as Hartshorne sees things (which works against Rorty's claim that there is an implicit drive toward epistemological *certainty* in Hartshorne), but it is not implausible that these individuals be seen as authoritative in *some* sense. By way of contrast, in a posthumously published article that appeared in 2001 (written in 1987), Hartshorne sings a slightly different tune, or at least he sings the same tune in a different pitch. He says not only that he personally has not had the sort of experiences that the religious mystics have claimed to have, but also that his faith relies primarily on metaphysical arguments, including the ontological argument (Hartshorne 2001, 255; 1984b, 5). It is precisely this sort of language that plays into Rorty's claim regarding the overemphasis of the formal and the necessary in Hartshorne.

Taken in isolation, there is no doubt that there are comments in Hartshorne's writings that support Rorty's judgment. But a reticulative effort to understand Hartshorne's philosophy as a whole makes Rorty's judgment problematic. At one point Hartshorne says that we perhaps ought to devote more of our time to meditation and less to rationalistic metaphysics, even though there is at present no vast amount of the latter (Hartshorne 1976). Also consider the fact that two of Hartshorne's many books are themselves works in the empirical sciences: *The Philosophy and Psychology of Sensation* (1934) in psychology and *Born to Sing* (1973) in ornithology. Or again, Hartshorne, in his 1929 review of Heidegger's *Being and Time* (the very first review of it in the English language), rejects the abstractness of Husserl's phenomenology and claims that Heidegger was less likely than Husserl to describe experience in terms of abstract phenomena like consciousness or intentionality, and more likely to describe it in terms of more concrete phenomena like feeling, willing, valuing, desiring, loving, and hating.

In this regard, Hartshorne thinks that the American pragmatists are even more successful than Heidegger. The specific achievement of the pragmatists, on this view, is their ironic critique of the British empiricists as not being sufficiently empirical. Hartshorne would have us turn the tertiary qualities of the British empiricists (e.g., color sensations, desires, etc.) into the primary ones. The primary qualities of the British empiricists (e.g., extension) are highly abstract and are ultimately derived from our experience of the "tertiary" ones (Dombrowski 1996a; 2004, Ch. 5). In short, there is much evidence from Hartshorne's writings that militates against Rorty's claim that the formal and the necessary dominate his philosophy, despite the fact that Hartshorne defends belief in the necessary existence of God through the ontological argument.

Necessary Truth

None of what I have said thus far is meant to hide the crucial role for the formal and the necessary in Hartshorne's philosophy, a role that is crucial in his defense of the ontological argument. Hartshorne thinks that three alternatives exhaust the logical possibilities: (1) there are no necessary truths; (2) there are necessary truths, but we cannot in principle know them; and (3) there are necessary truths and it makes sense for us to try to know them. Alternative (1), Hartshorne thinks, means not only that "necessary" has no application, but also that both this term and "contingent" lose their meaning. That is, the two terms are correlative and can only be defined in terms of each other. Likewise, if (2) is correct we have huge problems in that, on this alternative, when we speak not only of necessary truths, but also of contingent truths, we would not know what we are talking about, again on the Hartshornian assumption that "necessary" and "contingent" are correlative terms (Hartshorne 1995, 17–20).

Alternative (3) is the most credible position, Hartshorne thinks, not only because it points us toward those features that would have to be found in any possible world (necessary truths), but also because it helps us to secure an understanding of the contingent. Necessary truths (including the necessary truth found in the conclusion of the ontological argument) have gotten a bad name, he thinks, due to certain mistakes that have plagued the history of philosophy. One of these is the assumption that necessary truths have to concern (Boethian) eternal realities that are outside of time altogether, rather than everlasting realities that endure through all of time. Hartshorne's view is that "the eternal" is so abstract that it cannot have relations with (at least not internal relations with) that which becomes. Another mistake that has given necessary truths a bad name concerns a confusion between the necessity of a proposition and our knowledge of it. Our knowledge of a necessary truth (e.g., knowledge of the conclusion of the ontological argument), if we have such, is not itself necessary, as some like Rorty have mistakenly supposed.

A third mistake is the dangerous assumption that if one does know necessary truth one can then deduce contingent truths from the necessary ones. (We will see in an examination of Mark Taylor's thought that Hegel makes this mistake in his use of the ontological argument.) But this would end not only creaturely creativity, but process itself. Even with knowledge of necessary truths under one's belt one would still have to await the outcome of contingent events, Hartshorne thinks. It is one thing to know *that* a decision (literally, a cutting off of possibilities) must be made, another to know which decision. Or again, it is one thing to know *that* God exists necessarily, another to know *how* God exists in concrete detail from moment to moment.

Future Contingency

If God's knowledge of the creatures, for example, is a type of prehension, a feeling of the creatures' feelings, then it would not be possible for God to exhaustively know the future feelings of creatures if they depend on (at least partially) free decisions not yet made. Aristotle's view of the issue in his famous sea battle example seems to have been that propositions concerning future contingents are neither true nor false, but indeterminate. The main flaw of this view, which Hartshorne found attractive in the 1930s, is that it violates the law of excluded middle. As a result, this view will have to be challenged if we are to understand what God's knowledge of the future might mean and hence what a neoclassical defense of the ontological argument might mean.

From the 1940s until his death, however, Hartshorne held a different view wherein the law of excluded middle is not violated. The indeterminacy of the future is to be represented not in the truth value of propositions, but in three different predicates relating to the future itself (*de re* modality, rather than *de dictu*). For example, for any event causal conditions either *require* it (will be), *exclude* it (will not be), or *leave it undecided* (may or may not be). These three alternatives exhaust the logical possibilities. If any one of these is true of the event, the other two are false, hence the preservation of the law of excluded middle. The region of "may or may not be" is quite large in Hartshorne's philosophy, even for God, and cannot be reduced to "will be" or "will not be" merely by virtue of knowledge of *some* truths that are necessary, as in the truth that God exists necessarily (Hartshorne 1939; and the excellent work by Shields and Viney 2003).

Hartshorne asks why we should give up "*all* efforts to satisfy" an understandable curiosity to decipher the necessary aspects of reality, "in contrast and relation to which the contingent and emergent aspects alone have their full sense and definition." The word "all" indicates that Hartshorne's appeal to the formal and the necessary is by no means unbridled, as Rorty suggests. In any event, Hartshorne admits that Rorty is a thinker of great subtlety and that, because universal agreement is not possible in any discipline within philosophy, including metaphysics and scholarship concerning the ontological argument, our efforts to persuade each other of what we take to be necessary truths have a quasi-Rortean character to them.

But this does not mean that we should succumb to Rorty's (Quine-like and Wittgenstein-inspired) belief that the modal distinction between the necessary and the contingent has nothing to do with the universe and everything to do with our own practices. Rorty correctly notes that Hartshorne sides with Saul Kripke and David Lewis in believing in real modalities that are not solely functions of epistemic practices. Rorty's siding with Quine and Wittgenstein in this matter is due to his underlying belief (if the foundational metaphor can be allowed) that "human history" is "the measure of all things." Human history, he thinks, is, on the one hand, a "swelling, unfinished poem" and, on the other, an "ultimate context." That is, metaphysics or religion or science are *not* the ultimate contexts (Rorty 1995, 35–36). We should note at this point that Rorty is here rejecting not only theistic metaphysics and the ontological argument, but also any sort of environmental stance that calls into question the anthropocentric dogma that human beings and their history are *the* central realities in the world.

Contra Essentialism

It should be emphasized that Hartshorne's attempts to defend belief in necessary truths are not to be equated with either the quest for dogmatic certainty or with essentialism. These attempts reflect a Popperian opposition to what Rorty says about some sort of integral connection between the presence of the formal and the necessary, and essentialism. Hartshorne responds to Rorty as follows:

Is human thinking a mirror of nature? If what is meant by mirror is a medium reflecting with absolute distinctness and precision, then of course the human mind is no mirror. (Nor is an ordinary mirror that.) But if the criteria for mirroring are suitably relaxed, why is one's mind not analogously a mirror? I find no very impressive argument in Rorty on this point. Consider a geographical map. It is not a correspondent to its region with infinite precision or without qualification. But it is roughly, and for some purposes sufficiently, thus correspondent. (Hartshorne 1995, 25)

This view is, in a peculiar way, Popperian precisely because it involves commitment to the belief that, even if we cannot capture the essences of things, or capture the essence of God, we can nonetheless eliminate erroneous views concerning God and the creatures. Hartshorne's lifelong criticisms of classical theism and of the metaphysics of changeless being are prime examples of such error elimination. In effect, we can back our way into a picture of the world that is "more nearly correspondent with the realities" (Hartshorne 1995, 25). It will be remembered that this effort to reconcile perspectivalism, with its falsification capabilities, with realism was what Rorty admired in process philosophy in 1963 before he equated *any* sort of commitment to realism both with essentialism and with the view of philosophy as an ultra-precise mirror of nature.

Hartshorne states his contrasting view succinctly:

The two extremes – we know exactly what things are, and we know nothing of what they are – are both unjustified. If Rorty's view is not the second extreme, it is not easy to see the distinction. Some people set great store by the goal of not believing too much, others on not believing too little. Here, as everywhere, I am chronically a moderate and distrust extremes. My admiration for Popper arises partly from his avoidance of at least many extremes. In distrust of metaphysics he is less extreme than the positivists but still too extreme for my taste. (Hartshorne 1995, 25)

Here we can see a major difference between Popper's de-emphasis (but not elimination) of metaphysics and Rorty's utter disdain for this discipline. Popper is at least committed to the project of getting things right, to use Rorty's language, or at least to the project of not getting them wrong, and he is willing to consult metaphysicians when they enable us to make progress in this effort, for example, when they facilitate further investigation on the part of scientists by providing them with a roadmap of the conceptual terrain (Popper 1963). Rorty, by way of contrast, rejects metaphysics and the ontological argument as part of a general eschewal of the project of getting things right. Once again, he thinks of intellectual history not as an asymptotic approach to the truth, but as:

...a long, swelling, increasingly polyphonic poem – a poem that leads up to nothing save itself. When the species is extinct, "human nature's total message" will not be a set of propositions, but a set of vocabularies – the more, and the more various, the better. (Rorty 1995, 33)

The temperance of Hartshorne's approach to necessary truths can be seen in the fact that it is fallibilist in following Whitehead's famous metaphor in *Process and Reality*, where the true method of discovery is like the flight of a plane, starting from the ground of observation, taking flight in the air of imaginative generalization, and then landing for renewed observation and rational criticism (Whitehead 1978, 5). Rorty can bring Hartshorne within the sweep of his critique of metaphysics and the onto-logical argument only with the aid of caricature. He says that Hartshorne, along with Carnap, believes that everything that we do takes place "within an eternal, unchangeable framework" that we come in contact with via "an ideal language that pictures the way reality is in itself" (Rorty 1995, 33).

Or again, Rorty seems to think that Hartshorne continues the tradition that started with the ancient Greeks in believing that "nothing would ever change" because time was not worth taking seriously (Rorty 1995, 197). Not only is this an inaccurate summary of Hartshorne's asymmetrical view of time – wherein the past is already settled, but the future is yet to be determined, such that time *has to be* taken seriously – it also omits those aspects of Greek philosophy that prepared the way for Whitehead's and Hartshorne's process philosophies, most notably the "gignolatry" of Heraclitus and the later dialogues of Plato, where being is defined in terms of dynamic power (*dynamis* – *Sophist* 247E), and soul is defined in terms of self-motion (*Phaedrus* 245C, *Laws* X; also Dombrowski 2005).

Finding necessary truths is not the same as escaping from time and history, as many scholars of the ontological argument assume. We have seen that Hartshorne prefers the term "everlastingness" to "eternity," and if the latter term is used (rarely) he makes it clear that he is referring to the most abstract aspects of cosmic history and of becoming. Ultimacy is to be found not in an eternal region outside of time, but in the ubiquity of creativity, even at the microscopic level. Our knowledge of the ultimate, however, is not itself ultimate. Hartshorne's snappy way to put the point is to say that: "If we manage to arrive at a correct view of the necessary, this is a contingent achievement" (Hartshorne 1995, 17). Just as mistakes can occur in a highly abstract discipline like mathematics, they can also be made in metaphysics and regarding the ontological argument. Only God can have infallible knowledge of necessary truths. We are likely to make mistakes, especially by way of omission. In this regard Hartshorne's phi-losophy can be seen as changing the classical tradition of metaphysics by way of addition. Concepts like "being" and "absoluteness" were insight-fully explored by classical theistic metaphysicians, but not so broader terms like "becoming" and "relationality." God, he thinks, is immutably mutable, the greatest conceivable being who forever becomes.

Douglas Pratt puts the point as follows: "Hartshorne appears almost Hegelian in his desire for a higher synthesis by which his concept of God embraces both the thesis of classical theism and many of those views and positions which are normally taken to be antithetical to it" (Pratt 2002, 2). Conceptual change by way of addition is not to be confused with "foundationalism," the term that Rorty so often uses and that Hartshorne so often avoids. Indeed, Hartshorne insists that neither he nor Whitehead is a foundationalist in that "foundations" are sought by philosophers who are primarily interested in the problems invented by philosophers, rather than by the problems and experiences of human beings, including religious problems and religious experiences. But it is not enough to respond to these problems by "coping, merely coping" in that even insects cope quite well, Hartshorne notices. The question is: how close does our coping get us to an accurate and aesthetically satisfying view of reality, including divine reality? (Hartshorne 1995, 22, 24).

Nancarrow's Thesis

Nonetheless, we should not give up on the possibility of some sort of rapprochement between Rorty and Hartshorne, as I have indicated. In the debate between Hartshornian/Whiteheadian/Popperian realism and Rortean antirealism, we should notice that the former includes elements of correspondence *and* coherence theories of truth, as carefully argued by Paul Nancarrow (Nancarrow 1995). Rorty is correct that in some sense social practices come before ideas, as in the airplane metaphor from Whitehead, but this is a far cry from claiming, as Rorty does, that ideas are merely rhetorical ornaments. That is, some ideas enable us not only to cope better, but also to better avoid inaccurate descriptions of the world, as in the description of God's existence as contingent. Of course Rorty's response to the process view is that because we can never grasp what is out there really apart from our concepts and words, there is no foundation or even independent viewpoint from which we can compare our concepts and words with reality. We only have the concepts and words, he thinks. Objectivity is nothing but intersubjectivity, on this view (Rorty 1994; Nancarrow 1995, 61).

Nancarrow's generous and perceptive summary of Rorty's view is as follows:

For the anti-realist... the proposition "There is a mountain over there" is true when in some way "it pays" to speak in that manner, when asserting the proposition results in increased convenience or effectiveness or social utility or intersubjective agreement. To be sure, one of the things it pays to say about mountains is that they are there even when we're not making propositions about them; but the reason it pays has nothing to do with the mountain, but with the coherence of the propositions, the usefulness of the talking, the rules of the language-game in which "the mountain" is involved. (Nancarrow 1995, 62)

Process thought can reach some sort of rapprochement with Rorty's view by articulating a certain compatibility between the correspondence theory of truth and the coherence theory, by providing a middle path between simple-minded realism (a realism that illegitimately rejects perspectivalism, as Rorty rightly emphasizes) and an antirealism even more radical than Rorty's (although Rorty can be saved from this extreme stance only by appeal to his 1963 desire to reconcile perspectivalism and realism). This compatibility can be seen when a certain proposition like "There is a mountain over there" (to use Nancarrow's example, rather than the more complex example of the necessary existence of God) coheres with other experiences of the perceiver *and* when the experienced mountain to some degree corresponds with what is objectively present in the world at the time of the experience.

Process realism is not simple-minded precisely because of the relationality in process thought that Rorty commended in his early years. Rather than realistic portraiture, Whitehead and Hartshorne offer us interpretive abstraction. The mountain, on Nancarrow's analysis of process thinkers, is an abstraction from a richer, more detailed field of social relations. The proto-experiences at the microscopic level found *in* rocks, for example, may feel the strain of glacial ice on one part of the mountain more immediately than they do the feeling of being part of the mountain as a whole. Likewise, for some incipient experiences at the microscopic level *in* rocks (but not the rock as a whole, which, lacking a central nervous system, is insentient) there may be feelings of relatedness with reality more general than the mountain, as in the vague feeling of being part of a tectonic plate that stretches across continents. The concept "mountain" is highly abstract and can be seen as supporting many other societies of actual occasions. To speak simply of "the mountain" is to omit a great deal of detail. This is not the sort of realism that Rorty rejects because a proposition (about the mountain, say) does not so much picture its subject as it interprets it (Nancarrow 1995, 65–66).

Nancarrow is correct to suggest that whereas Rorty forces a choice between truth-as-correspondence and truth-as-coherence, process thinkers like Whitehead and Hartshorne include both of them as parts of a thoroughly relational (i.e., nonfoundational) view of the world. The ideal is some sort of reflective equilibrium or harmony between the two such that when coherence is lost we begin to wonder whether our theories really do tell us about the way things are; and when our ideas are resisted by the world we begin to wonder why most of us hold on to them. (Regarding the latter it should be noted that to say *that* God exists necessarily, without claiming *how* God exists, we have not said anything that could conflict with the rest of the world.) But if we are given the forced choice between the two by Rorty, many thinkers are rightly tempted to choose truth-as-correspondence over truth-as-coherence because of a legitimate fear that their intellectual contact with the real world would otherwise be lost, thereby giving the impression that they are simple-minded realists. The wise move, however, is to resist the forced choice (Nancarrow 1995, 67).

The mountain may support (as in the aforementioned glacial ice), or be supported by (as in the aforementioned plate tectonics), an indefinite number of interrelated societies, such that "the mountain" is itself an abstraction from them. But this does not mean that the mountain is caused by the percipient, nor that the mountain is an "artifact of the percipient's language-games," to use Nancarrow's characterization of Rorty's position. As before, propositions about the mountain are true not when they accurately *picture* it, but when they accurately *interpret* it in light of its place in various nested societies that are interrelated. I think that this is the best way to understand Hartshorne's (and Popper's) example of the relative accuracy of geographic maps. Interpretive accuracy, however, should not be seen solely in cognitive terms in that propositions, for Hartshorne as well as for Whitehead, are also lures for *feeling*. It may very well be that the *truth* of a proposition depends on its correspondence to reality from some interpretive standpoint or other, but its *importance* requires its coherence with what gives us enjoyment and with our other purposes (Nancarrow 1995, 66–67).

In fact, it seems that truth is to be valued *because* it contributes to the adaptation of our experiences, to their harmonization in a beautiful life. Whitehead went so far as to say that "a true proposition is more apt to be interesting than a false one" and that "Truth matters because of Beauty" (Whitehead 1961, 244, 267). Even if there is something hyperbolic in the way that Whitehead makes this latter point (consider Hartshorne's general agreement with, and emphasis on, Tarski's view of truth), the general insight here that aesthetic concerns impinge on epistemological and ethical ones is enough to cast into doubt Rorty's claim that we must choose between truth-as-correspondence and truth-as-coherence, between truth as traditionally understood (and as presupposed in the ontological argument) and importance, and between epistemology and metaphysics, and aesthetics, respectively. Nonetheless the partial sub-servience of truth (as correspondence) to beauty (conceived as the mutual adaptation and harmonization of the different elements of expe-rience) in process thought can be seen as analogous to Rorty's claim that correspondence is secondary to coherence. So far, so good. Unfortu-nately, Rorty attenuates the secondary status of truth-as-correspondence to the vanishing point (Nancarrow 1995, 68–69).

Rorty is correct, from a Hartshornian point of view, that we talk about mountains because it pays to do so in terms of aesthetic enhancement of our experience ("The mountain is sublime at dusk"), the fulfillment of ethical responsibilities ("Clearcut logging of the mountain ought to be resisted"), and the fostering of intersubjectivity ("We can all share in the grandeur of the mountain") (Nancarrow 1995, 70). But all of these are only possible because of *the fact that* there is a mountain. As Nancarrow puts the point: success in the pattern of correspondence eventually leads to "a new accession of coherence," which makes the pattern more sophis-ticated, in turn leading to greater success at correspondence, and so on. Scientific "revolutions" in the short run should not prevent us from notic-ing with a wide-angle lens this interplay between the correspondence and coherence aspects of truth, an interplay entirely absent in the later Rorty (Nancarrow 1995, 73), although present in the early Rorty where creative process is seen as the stage for deciding which abstract possibilities will be actualized in the real world so as to produce "the greatest subjective intensity of enjoyment" (Rorty 1963a, 516). All of this is important here because *some* sort of resuscitation of truth as correspondence is required for the ontological argument to go through.

Despite Rorty's explicit rejection of metaphysics and the ontological argument, he is like many analytic philosophers in adopting an implicit metaphysical materialism. On this point Hartshorne finds Rorty to be either "crude or dogmatic"; science, which Rorty sees as our most reliable guide regarding the natural world, has moved away from the classical view in physics of absolute laws governing a reductionistic materialist world. Scientists now indicate that chance is a real factor in all processes such that valid scientific laws are not absolute but statistical in character. As is well known, Hartshorne defends a version of panpsychism. Not so well known is the fact that Hartshorne does not deny, as Rorty alleges he denies, that neural processes are physical events. The question, once dualism is rejected (both Rorty and Hartshorne are in favor of such a rejection), is whether physical events are best described in terms of inert, lifeless, completely determined material stuff (an implicit metaphysics that leaves the world as unintelligible as it is found, according to Peirce), *or* in terms of active singulars, partially self-moving pulses of physical activity, which enable us to understand both causal regularity *and* the chance elements in nature (Hartshorne 1995, 20, 22; Rorty 1979, 116–117).

Panpsychism (or psychicalism, as Hartshorne labels it) is not the view that *psyche* is a special kind of reality, but rather that it just is reality itself. *Psyche* here refers not necessarily to mind or soul, but to Platonic self-motion of some sort that is not always conscious of itself as such. Nor is panpsychism the view that the "mental" and the "physical" are two aspects of the same reality, as Rorty alleges. There are two problems with Rorty's interpretation here. First, this sounds more like Spinoza than Hartshorne. And second, "*psyche*" is a much broader term than "mind" (although it includes mind) that refers to *any* sort of proto-sentient soul/mind/experience/self-motion, even what is found in subatomic particles. As Hartshorne puts the point: "It is mind that knows (other) mind, experience that discloses (other) experience. Mere matter is an empty negation that explains nothing" (Hartshorne 1995, 23). Of course a teapot, to use Hartshorne's example, does not experience anything as a whole, but "the molecules and atoms into which physics analyzes teapots are not nearly so different in certain essential respects" from experiences, in general, nor from us, in particular (Hartshorne 1995, 23).

Hartshorne thinks that Peirce was the discoverer of the statistical notion of causal order, with little help from the scientists of his day outside of those working on the kinetic theory of gases. Since the advent of quantum mechanics, however, this view of causal order is more widely accepted (Malin 2001). If causal order were absolute, then real possibilities regarding the future would be paradoxical. In fact, on this basis "possibility" would presumably refer merely to our ignorance of what was already in the cards. At the other extreme, if there were no causal order at all, "the entire . . . realm of the thinkable could also be really available for tomorrow's happenings" (Hartshorne 1963a, 599–600). But then the words "real possibility" would lose their usefulness, a loss that would have an effect on the ontological argument in that the argument depends on a clear distinction between necessity and possibility (whether logical or real). In fact, thinking itself would lose its usefulness because no intelligent preparation for the future would make any sense because *anything* could happen next. The view that *does* make sense is the intermediate, pragmatist one (but not Rorty's version of pragmatism, with its implicit materialist metaphysics) wherein "causal laws are limited to an approximate or statistical validity" (Hartshorne 1963a, 600).

In short:

Deny causality, and the tiny range of the causally available possibilities for the immediate future instantly expands into the featureless immensities of the merely logically possible. Assert absolute or classical determinism, and the "range" of available possibilities is no longer even a range, but shrinks to a point, one uniquely definite possibility for each region of space-time. . . . Law and chance are twin aspects of real modality, and neither is ever found alone. (Hartshorne 1963a, 601)

Strictly speaking, there are no such things as future events, only possibilities or probabilities for future becoming. Rorty's flirtation with materialism leads one to wonder whether he should, in order to be consistent, also flirt with determinism in that it is not clear what the sources of freedom or creaturely escape from material regularity would be (Rorty 1979, 114–115).

By contrast, Hartshorne is quite explicit regarding his own rejection of both reductionistic materialism and determinism:

"Possibility" is creativity in its forward or productive aspect; "actuality" is the same in its backward or preservative aspect. Logical modalities express the ways in which creatures may understand their situations as heirs of a definite past and as contributors to future creatures which are definite in advance only with respect to the contributions that will be at their disposal. (Hartshorne 1963a, 605)

Wordsworth

I would like to make clearer the meaning of the title of the present chapter. We have seen that Rorty refers to human history, in contrast to the region of "eternal" truth that he opposes, as a vast poem. This is a clue that indicates that the word "poetry" and its cognates are used in a wide sense in Rorty so as to include even the conversations constructed by "the much-footnoted Plato," if not the metaphysical claims, including the implicit ontological argument, made in these conversations. In response to William James, Rorty distinguishes between two sorts of poetry: one that involves a Whitmanesque expansion of the wider self so as to glimpse "the farthest reach of the democratic vistas"; and another that includes a Wordsworthian "over-belief" in something "far more deeply interfused with nature than the transitory glory of democratic fellowship." Admittedly, the options presented by these two romantic poets – Whitman and

Wordsworth – are not exactly those of atheism and theistic metaphysics, respectively. *If* these were the choices presented to us, however, Rorty would obviously choose Whitmanesque atheism and Hartshorne would choose Wordsworthian theism buttressed by the ontological argument (Rorty 1999, 163–164; 1995, 211).

Both Rorty and Hartshorne are admirers of Wordsworth, even if there is a difference of opinion between them regarding how to assess Wordsworth's contribution. Hartshorne finds Wordsworth helpful in the effort to articulate metaphysical positions such as panpsychism and theism. Regarding the former, he agrees with Wordsworth that with effort we can see "into the life of things" (Hartshorne 1995, 24; Wordsworth 1981, "Tintern Abbey"; Rorty 1995, 31). And, regarding theism, Hartshorne finds Wordsworth's language of something being "far more deeply interfused" into nature extremely helpful in enabling us to conceive of necessary existence. Rorty is thankful that Hartshorne alerted him to this moving passage in Wordsworth while he was an undergraduate:

> And I have felt
> A presence that disturbs me with the joy
> Of elevated thoughts; a sense sublime
> Of something far more deeply interfused.
> (Wordsworth 1981, "Tintern Abbey")

But it is the *poetry* of Wordsworth, stripped of all metaphysical claims, that he loves. Hartshorne's Wordsworth, he alleges, is mixed in with logical proofs of necessary truths, especially the ontological argument, which Rorty thinks is like mixing oil and water, or combining the spirit of Grasmere Lake with that of Whitehead's and Russell's *Principia Mathematica* (Rorty 1995, 30).

Because Rorty is skeptical as to whether we could ever know the way things are in themselves, he believes we have no way of knowing whether Democritus or Lucretius or J. J. C. Smart, on the one hand, or Wordsworth or Whitehead or Hartshorne, on the other, are more likely to help us reach the goal of an accurate description of the way things are. And no doubt Rorty is correct that some people *do* distort poetry for the sake of metaphysics. However, it is also possible that stripping poetry of its metaphysical implications will distort and impoverish it.

I think that one would be correct to suspect a stacked deck here. Rorty is quick to state that we ought not to choose between competing metaphysical schemes at least in part because "convergence to a single set of metaphysical or religious opinions" is not even desirable. But *why* is such a convergence undesirable, one might ask, as long as it is not the result of coercion? Both Whitehead and Hartshorne were political liberals, it should be remembered, and shared many of Rorty's political goals regarding the importance of freedom and emancipation from political servitude, poverty, and ignorance (Morris 1991).

In effect, Rorty thinks that Wordsworth does not need to be backed up by metaphysical arguments. Presumably, we need not think about what sort of feelings Wordsworth has in mind when we read Wordsworth say that:

> The budding twigs spread out their fan,
> To catch the breezy air;
> And I must think, do all I can,
> That there was pleasure there.
> (Wordsworth 1981, "Lines Written in Early Spring")

Hartshorne, by way of contrast, *is* interested in this topic, which he thinks is at the core of what Wordsworth is writing about. He has us notice that Wordsworth has the pleasure in the twigs, not in the tree as a whole, which, lacking a central nervous system, is not sentient as a whole. It is a metaphysical democracy, to use Whitehead's language. That is, the "twigs" are metaphors for the microscopic constituents of the tree (Rorty 1998, 290–291). Likewise, Rorty is not led to think about divinity in the "far more deeply interfused" character of nature. He succinctly puts the point, simultaneously regarding the supremacy of Whitehead and Hartshorne as metaphysicians and the overall poverty of metaphysics: "I think of metaphysicians as footnotes to poets. . . . I think that, as footnotes to Wordsworth go, Whitehead and Hartshorne write the best ones. But I prefer Wordsworth unfootnoted" (Rorty 1995, 32).

Rather than participating in the life of things, Rorty wants to participate in the life of Wordsworth. To see the contrast in another way, consider the following from Rorty:

Hartshorne wants to make the world safe for Wordsworth metaphysically, and I want to do the same thing metaphilosophically. He wants to argue that some of what Wordsworth said is literally, philosophically, metaphysically true – that Wordsworth got something right. I want to argue that we can get the most out of Wordsworth by not asking whether he got anything right. (Rorty 1995, 32)

On this basis, the title of the present chapter is appropriate: the ultimate dispute between Rorty and Hartshorne concerns the split between poetry (as Rorty uses the term) and metaphysics, especially the ontological argument. However, one cannot help but wonder about what is left of

Wordsworth when the life of things is turned into a life*less* abstraction and when the something "far more deeply interfused" into matter is excised. By excising the very things that animated Wordsworth, both he and his life's work are left as inanimate shells of their former "glory in the flower" (Wordsworth 1981, "Intimations of Immortality").

"We murder to dissect," as Wordsworth famously put it (Wordsworth 1981, "The Tables Turned"). It is ironic that an elegant writer like Rorty has misunderstood *both* metaphysics and poetry.

3

Deconstructionism and the Ontological Argument

The Case of Mark Taylor

The Viability of Philosophy

Let us start with a quotation from Mark Taylor:

> Hegel brings to systematic completion insights anticipated by Plotinus and Augustine and subsequently articulated by Anselm. The entire Hegelian edifice can actually be understood as a sustained argument for God's existence. Anselm's faith seeking understanding becomes Hegel's translation of religious *Vorstellungen* into the philosophical *Begriffe*. Inasmuch as Hegel's system marks the closure of the ontotheological tradition, his philosophical rendering of the ontological argument is a pivotal moment in the fulfillment of the Western philosophical quest. If the ontological argument is in any way inadequate, ontotheology inevitably fails. Thus, philosophy's stake in the ontological argument is nothing less than the viability of philosophy itself. (Taylor 1993, 11–12; 1982, 34–40)

These remarkable lines were written in 1993 by Taylor, who is at present perhaps the most important deconstructionist philosopher of religion and theologian (or better, as he puts it, a/theologian). I say that these lines are "remarkable" despite the fact that no one, as far as I know, has yet remarked on them. Taylor has gone on to write more books and to say even more arresting things, but I think it may profit us to slow down the speed of Taylor's cinematic career so as to carefully examine a part of this single frame, which, if I understand Taylor correctly, implicitly contains the following argument:

A. If the ontological argument fails (O) then the ontotheological tradition that culminates in Hegel fails (OT).
B. If the ontotheological tradition that culminates in Hegel fails (OT) then philosophy itself is no longer viable (P).

C. The ontological argument fails because it negates every vestige of divine alterity, and so on (O).

D. Therefore, philosophy is no longer viable (P).

This argument is formally valid, but it is not, I think, sound. It is not sound because, as I see things, all three premises are false.

The argument can be stated more formally as follows:

A. O → OT.

B. OT → P.

C. O.

D. ∴ P.

A brief comment on the first and second premises should be enough to cast doubt on the soundness of the argument. I will spend most of my time commenting on the third premise, concerning which I will allege that if the ontological argument does, in fact, fail, it is not due to anything Taylor says by way of criticism of that argument. That is, I hope to refute Taylor's own argument in this chapter; or, at the very least, I hope to show by way of careful examination of Taylor's dismissal of the ontological argument, and by way of a defense of the thought of Hartshorne, the viability of philosophy. In this regard I will be criticizing Taylor's views in a way similar to David Ray Griffin (Griffin 1989a, 29–61; cf. Johnson 1998).

Before examining these premises, however, I should say a few words about what Taylor means by philosophy not being "viable." It may be the case, as Viney has pointed out to me, that Taylor's belief regarding the nonviability of philosophy is close to Rorty's proposal that we replace philosophy (and science) with poetry. Or again, and perhaps more appropriately in that Taylor is an a/theologian, the nonviability of philosophy might have something to do with his apophaticism. On this interpretation, Taylor is engaging in a sort of Wittgensteinian pointing, rather than a saying, a *poesis* rather than a *logos*. In any event, Taylor himself leaves the nonviability of philosophy in an ambiguous state.

The first premise is problematic because many theists (e.g., St. Thomas Aquinas, Richard Swinburne) rationally defend belief in God – or, as Taylor puts it, belief in the ontotheological tradition – on grounds other than the ontological argument. Taylor needs to argue for the first premise and cannot assume without argument that it is true. (Later I will examine a gesture toward a defense of the first premise in Taylor.) Nor can he assume without argument, as he apparently does, that Kant is correct that all of the arguments for God's existence collapse into the ontological one, such that if the latter fails they all fail. Kant's view of this matter is highly controversial, especially among some of those who see the arguments for the existence of God as mutually reinforcing (Peircian) strands in a cable.

The second premise is problematic because Taylor has not offered an argument showing why philosophy's viability depends on the viability of the ontotheological tradition. Presumably what he has in mind is that if the universe is not centered in God then the centered self disintegrates as well, and, as a result, epistemological and moral criteria disintegrate. But some philosophers (e.g., Jean-Paul Sartre, Karl Popper) do not believe in God. It is by no means clear, however, why that fact alone should disqualify them from engaging in a viable intellectual activity called "philosophy." Or, if I am mistaken about this, then an argument is required to this effect from Taylor rather than the assumption without argument that the second premise is true.

Before moving to the third premise, which is my prime concern, I should respond to the criticism I am sure to receive to the effect that by attributing an argument to Taylor, and by proposing a counterargument, I have misunderstood what his "philosophy" or "theology" are all about (the scare quotes are needed because both of these are nonviable, on Taylor's terms).

The issue is complex, however. Deconstructionists themselves legitimately press at least two points that are crucial for the development of any defensible argument: nothing that a human being can put into words can give *the final answer* to any question of real importance; and the attempt to make *ultimate* sense verbally carries with it the danger of oppressive or totalitarian conceptual schemes. For both of these points the deconstructionists should be thanked, although it seems to me that many great philosophers (e.g., Peirce, Whitehead, Popper, Hartshorne) have written (and presumably lived) as if they were in agreement with these points. To grant these two points is not to grant that we cannot make intellectual progress, at the very least by ameliorating our most egregious errors, nor that there is no point in criticizing the arguments we or others make.

Consider the quotation from Taylor that opened this chapter. He is trying here and elsewhere to convince us of something, that philosophy of religion and theology are not viable (his conclusion), and he is willing to use various techniques, rational or otherwise, to persuade us to see things the way he does. One can grant the above two points and still think it worthwhile to keep Taylor, or anyone else who solicits our intellectual attention, honest.

To be frank, the quotation from Taylor strikes me as hyperbolic and a bit too histrionic, and hence it is in need of criticism. And one cannot take

Taylor off the hook by "situating" him within a tradition where hyperbole and histrionics seem to be acceptable. Perhaps the tradition is also in need of criticism. For example, in Nietzsche's second or positivistic period, where he entertained the possibility that science would resolve the issues that religion had previously resolved, and give meaning to life just as religion had previously done, he considered himself to be practicing a philological-philosophical science; indeed, he refers to his own work as "the greatest triumph" of the history of science!, an estimation that is as bothersome to those who are familiar with the history of science as it is to religious believers (Nietzsche 1984, 16; Taylor 1980).

In short, we should welcome the deconstructionists' warning regarding the hegemonic dangers associated with certain philosophic or theological discourse. But there seems to be no alternative for those who think that we can make mistakes, or that we can exaggerate – in the fashion of Nietzsche and Taylor – to the back and forth movement in philosophy and theology of argument and counterargument. These are the means by which we can, at best, asymptotically approach the truth, or, at the very least, approach a reflective equilibrium of the intellectual forces at work at any particular time. By way of contrast, we should note Taylor's performative self-contradiction, to use Griffin's designation. One engages in a performative self-contradiction when one offers arguments to the effect that arguments are of no use.

I would now like to examine Taylor's support for the third premise. His view in his book titled *nOts* is that the Western ontotheological tradition has been an extended effort "not to think not." That is, any arguments for the existence of, or attempts to name, God are always inadequate. This is unfortunate because "the not is a matter of life and death." (By the way, this strikes me as yet another hyperbolic claim in need of explication by Taylor.) Of course, St. Anselm and Hegel and others who defend the ontological argument admit that God is *not* like human beings, but they inevitably "erase the not" despite the apparent success of the *via nega-tiva* "to think not." The classical *via negativa* or apophatic religious language remains thoroughly ontotheological, according to Taylor, along with Derrida (Taylor 1993, 1–2).

Taylor admits, however, that the thinking about and naming of God, that is, theology, has achieved its greatest rigor in the ontological argument. But he thinks that the argument goes too far, despite the fact that it does not, as Taylor himself at one point notices, entail the *necessity* of thinking God. The whole argument, however, seems unnecessary, on Taylor's view (Taylor 1993, 11). His critique of the ontological argument relies more on Hegel's version of it, as articulated in his *Lectures on the Philosophy of Religion*, than on Anselm's version(s). It is crucial, he thinks, that for Hegel this argument is actually an appendix to his logic. Or better, all three arguments that he offers constitute a single complex proof which, in turn, constitutes such an appendix. The cosmological part of the proof corresponds to the religion of nature, the teleological to the religion of spiritual individuality, and the ontological to that of absolute religion: the single proof moves from nature to spirit to the absolute. Or again, the cosmological part establishes God's power, the teleological part establishes God's wisdom, and the ontological part establishes God as Absolute Idea. Or, as Taylor puts the point in *Deconstructing Theology*, the first two moments in the proof progress from the world to God – the *Itinerarium Mentis in Deum* – and the ontological moment moves from the idea of God to God's existence – *Descensus Dei im Mundi* – hence Hegel comes full circle (Taylor 1982).

Taylor's fascination with Hegel is, in part, responsible for his belief that defenders of the ontological argument bite off more than they can chew: in Hegel (in contrast to Hartshorne, for example) the ontological argument does not merely demonstrate the necessary *existence* of God; rather, when fully realized as the Absolute Idea, "the concept is the all-encompassing totality that constitutes all existence. To think properly or truly is to think all things in God and God in all things" (Taylor 1993, 20). We will see that Hartshorne's version of the ontological argument is not nearly as ambitious as Hegel's, and hence it is not as amenable to Taylor's deconstructionist downsizing.

The failure of Hegel's use of the ontological argument is rooted in Anselm's failure as well, according to Taylor, who anachronistically has Anselm asking the question, "How not to think God?" Taylor is ambivalent on this point. Previously we have seen him say that it is not necessary that we think God in Anselm, but now it seems he is alleging that in Anselm "it is impossible to avoid thinking God." Once again, it is unfortunate that he does not even mention contemporary defenders of the ontological argument like Hartshorne (or Alvin Plantinga, et al.), who have made painstaking efforts to clear up these and other confusions regarding the ontological argument. That is, it is not the case that for a defender of the ontological argument "the only way not to think God is not to think" (Taylor 1993, 11, 23, 25).

More bothersome, however, is another instance of hyperbole when Taylor says that "in the presence of philosophical knowledge, every vestige of alterity is negated." However, a defense of the ontological argument is quite compatible with a robust sense of alterity or the *via negativa* or apophatic divine discourse. And an intelligent response can be given to Taylor's question, which I assume is not merely rhetorical: "Is the thinking of God inevitable or impossible?" Taylor's own response to this question seems to be that, if God is "a name for the unnameable," then it is impossible to think of God. It is precisely this aggressive use of the *via negativa* that is most bothersome in Taylor's view (Taylor 1993, 24, 26).

To sum up my argument thus far: Taylor thinks that the ontological argument fails because: it tries to accomplish too much by offering us a concept of the all-encompassing totality that seems to explain, at least implicitly, practically everything (but this expansive version of the ontological argument, though perhaps characteristic of Hegel's use of it, is definitely not Hartshorne's); it negates *every* (Taylor's word) vestige of divine alterity; and it makes it impossible not to think of God. And because the ontological argument fails, Taylor thinks (but why?) that the ontotheological tradition fails, which causes (but why?) philosophy itself to be unviable.

Religious Language

I would like to criticize the third premise of Taylor's implied argument, and I would like to do so by borrowing freely from Hartshorne, who can legitimately be seen as a *constructive* postmodern philosopher of religion or theologian who nonetheless defends the ontological argument (Griffin 1989a). Regarding religious language, Hartshorne urges that two extremes be avoided: on the one hand, that we can capture deity in some verbal formula devoid of any doubt or obscurity, as the deconstructionists rightly suggest, and, on the other, that we are totally in the dark regarding the effort to describe God. Three different uses of religious language will help us to get to the heart of the matter.

A. *Literal* terms applied to God do not deal with matters of degree, but deal with matters of all or none. That is, literal terms express a purely formal status by classifying propositions as of a certain logical type. For example, the categorical terms "absolute" and "relative" have a literal meaning when applied to God: either God is independent of (that is, is absolute with respect to) creatures for divine *existence* or is not. And either God is related to (that is, is relative to) creatures in the divine *actuality* or is not. God, for Hartshorne, is literally absolute in existence and relative in actuality or in the mode of divine existence. Or again, the ontological argument attempts to show that the fact that God exists is not dependent on us even if how God exists (divine actuality) *is* partially dependent on us.

B. *Analogical* terms applied to God, by way of contrast, admit of degree as they apply to different entities within the same logical type. For example, concrete individuals feel in different degrees of intensity and with different levels of adequacy, with God being the supreme example of feeling in that God is intensely affected by and affects all of reality.

C. Any *symbolic* terms applied to God are used locally and not cosmically to a particular kind of individual in a particular culture, with an even greater degree of specificity than analogical terms, as when God is referred to as a lightning bolt or a monarch.

There is an obvious distinction between formal and material predication. To compare God with a rock, a shepherd, or a parent is a material description that cannot be literal. Formal or nonmaterial predication is illustrated when one refers to God as absolute or relative. The formal (literal) predicates of deity, however, are not exclusively negative, as Taylor implies. If God's very existence cannot be contingent, as is claimed in the ontological argument, the question arises: is God's necessary existence to be conceived as having the ability to be related to creatures (indeed the *need* to be related to creatures) or simply as the absence of relativity? These are two categorically or formally opposite ways of interpreting the proposition "God exists." On either interpretation something literal is being said of God. In between the formal, literal terms (absolute-relative, being-becoming, etc.) and the most material, particular, symbolic ones (shepherd, monarch, lightning bolt, parent, etc.) there are analogical terms (love, knowledge, personality, etc.). To the extent that analogical terms involve qualitative distinctions of degree they are removed from the all-or-nothing character of literal terms. Who can say literally how divine love differs *qualitatively* from ours? That is, there is a certain amount of Hartshornian "silence" at work when analogical or especially symbolic religious language is used, hence Taylor is premature in urging that a defender of the ontological argument destroys divine alterity altogether.

It is also crucial that we distinguish between two different sorts of literal terms when they are applied to God. The first sort, as we have seen, refers to those abstract terms that describe God as exhibiting a certain logical type or not (literal-1). The second sense of "literal" refers, ironically enough, to a certain distinction within the use of analogical terms (literal-2). It is a commonplace in philosophy of religion that we start with human experience and then analogize regarding God. But once we reach some understanding of the concept of God (or have some sort of experience of God) the reverse path is also open. That is, there is a sense in which analogical terms apply literally-2 to God and only analogously to us. For example, strictly speaking, only God knows. We are said to "know" certain things, but we are always liable to make mistakes. The indefiniteness of our knowing is in contrast to the divine case (Dombrowski 1996b, 157–165).

Neither absoluteness nor relativity have been adequately understood by many theists, overly influenced as they often are by the tradition of negative theology. It is easy enough to say that one is being modest in claiming, as Taylor apparently does, that human language cannot properly apply to God, hence we cannot speak literally about God. But negative theology itself can be a sort of presumption. Dare we to forbid God to sustain relations with creatures and thus be influenced by them? Some traditional theists, along with Taylor, do precisely this, but not Hartshorne. When some traditional theists say that God may have relations with creatures symbolically, and in effect tell God that such relations cannot be literal, is this not monstrous presumption? Hartshorne, by way of contrast, does not try to exert this sort of veto power over God.

The modesty of a Taylor-like negative theology is somewhat suspect because it puts a human veto on the wealth of the divine life. We *should* be influenced by negative theology, but not exclusively so. We can speak literally about the fact that God is relative; that is, is related to (must be related to, if God is the greatest conceivable being-in-becoming) creatures. But we cannot speak literally about what it is like concretely to *be* God. Here we must remain somewhat silent. We can only speak of God in literal terms if we do so abstractly; we can only talk about what it is like to be God concretely in, at best, analogical terms. But if there is no sense whatsoever in which univocal meaning or literal terms can be used regarding God, then talk about God is pure sophistry.

The heavy influence of the *via negativa* on traditional theism has created the illusion of safety in what is not said regarding the description of God. But overly aggressive negative theologians like Taylor have typically atoned for their paucity of discourse by an orgy of symbols and metaphors (anyone who has read a great deal of Taylor's work understands the point). We should obviously not be opposed to symbolism; in fact, religious symbolism has a crucial role to play in moving the emotions toward God. But description of God must be based on *some* literal terms or it is a scandal. Analogy itself, as a comparison between things that are somewhat similar and somewhat different, ultimately rests on there being *some* univocity of discourse so as to secure the similarities. It is true, however, that the contingent or concrete actuality of God (as opposed to the abstraction "contingency" or the abstraction "concreteness") transcends reason and literal discourse in the sense that this reality must ultimately be felt as a sheer fact.

Thus, in response to the criticism that the neoclassical theist is claiming too much knowledge about God, we should urge the reverse. The knowledge claimed is very abstract. But what the divine life is like concretely is quite mysterious. It is one thing to know an individual as distinguished from other individuals. It is another thing to know that same individual in *its* actual mode of existence or in *its* actual state (e.g., as Bartók or as a bat or as a bacterium). To know deity in this sense is to know the universe as God knows it. Here, once again, we must maintain Hartshornian silence.

It should now be somewhat clear how we should respond to Taylor's critique of the ontological argument. First, this argument *does* try to accomplish too much in its Anselmian and especially in its Hegelian formats, where not only the mere existence of deity is demonstrated, but also divine actuality; too much information regarding how God must exist, the mode of God's actuality, is given in the Hegelian version. By failing to distinguish between existence and actuality, some defenders of the ontological argument have played into Taylor's hands, as when Hegel thinks he has demonstrated the Absolute Idea of an "all-encompassing totality." Second, of course, Taylor would also reject the Hartshornian version of the ontological argument. But why? Divine alterity is decidedly not eliminated, as Taylor alleges, when divine actuality – *how* God exists – is our concern. And, third, the Hartshornian version of the ontological argument does not state, as Taylor at one point alleges of ontological arguments in general, that it is necessary that we think of God if we think at all.

There are normally three options regarding the existence of a thing, as we have seen. First, the existence of a thing can be impossible, as in a square-circle or (due to temporal asymmetry) as in Jimi Hendrix now performing a protest song about George W. Bush. Second, the existence of a thing can be possible, but it does not in fact exist, as in an intelligent American president (it is 2004 as I write). And third, the existence of a thing can be possible, and in point of fact that being does exist. The point to the ontological argument is that, regarding God, the second option drops out, because to entertain this option is to no longer think about God – that than which no greater can be conceived – but about a lesser being-in-becoming whose existence is contingent.

In short, it is not *necessary* that we think of God, as Taylor alleges of defenders of the ontological argument, in that we can also think exclusively about things like a good pick-and-roll play or pretzels. But *if we do* think appropriately of the concept of God we have to think of God as existing necessarily. Two options are logically open to us: either it is impossible to think of the concept of God (positivism) or it is possible to think of the concept of God, in which case if and when we do think of the concept of God we must think of God as existing necessarily (theism). But the positivistic option here, defended by J. N. Findlay in his famous ontological disproof of the existence of God, indicates that Taylor is inaccurate when he attributes a hegemonic intent to defenders of the ontological argument (Findlay 1948). The one thing we cannot do, according to defenders of the ontological argument, is claim that we have legitimately considered God's existence as contingent; we cannot legitimately do this because it contradicts the very logic of perfection. *If* we can think of an unsurpassable being-in-becoming (unsurpassable except, perhaps, by itself at a later stage in the divine process), then it would have to exist necessarily. Belief in the necessary existence of God does not, however, have to lead to a totalizing concept in Levinas' sense, because in Hartshorne's neoclassical or process theism God's perfection is a *changing* one that never achieves totality.

Derrida's and Taylor's belief that the *via negativa* employed by traditional theists was really part of a positive theology is surely correct. But the way to adequately respond to traditional theism is not to defend an even more expansive version of the *via negativa*, as Taylor does. Rather, we should think through more carefully than either traditional theists or deconstructionists have done the complementary roles of the *via positiva* or kataphatic divine discourse, on the one hand, and the *via negativa* or apophatic divine discourse, on the other. Further, as we have seen, there is a crucial need to distinguish between divine existence (that God exists) and divine actuality (how God exists). Traditional theism is inextricably tied to negative theology, as when it commits itself to the claim that God does not change. But to put human beings in their proper place there is no need to allow them to usurp and exhaust categories like adaptation and change. This gives human beings undue importance, as Hartshorne indicates:

If Anselm's formula, "God is whatever it is better to be than not to be," had been strictly conformed to the negative theology, it would have run, "God is not what it is worse to be than not to be." Would this have improved it? I submit: we do not worship God because of the defects which He does not have. We worship Him for His positive and all-encompassing love and beauty. The use of the Argument by proponents of the negative or classical theology has not been a grand success. (Hartshorne 1965, 69; also 1970, 151 – it should be emphasized that Hartshorne later abandoned male pronouns when dealing with God)

These remarks apply, I think, in different ways, to Hegel as well as to Taylor.

When we say God is not literally a shepherd or a ruler or a potter, but is these things only symbolically, we are then using the *via negativa* in a moderate sense because a shepherd, a ruler, and a potter are very specific sorts of things. To "forbid" God to literally be a shepherd is not really to restrict divine perfection. The matter is quite different when we are dealing with abstract terms like "being" or "becoming," "absolute" or "relative":

There are not an infinity of miscellaneous possible positive forms of reality alternative to being relative; there is only being non-relative or absolute. If God is not literally finite and relative [in existence], then he is literally and exclusively infinite and absolute [in existence]. But there is no third possibility: here the law of excluded middle must...apply. (Hartshorne 1970, 152 – bracketed remarks added)

If God is not a shepherd, according to the *via negativa*, then God is free to be a super-shepherd, whatever that might be. But "super-relative" can only be understood as an eminent form of relatedness to others, of contingent relations to others.

To claim that God is necessary in existence but contingent in actuality (i.e., in the precise mode of existence) is to say that there is no symbolic way of existing necessarily (Hartshorne 1970, 153). In between literal terms and symbolic ones are psychic terms that denote states or functions very like the human, but not with the degree of specificity associated with "shepherd" or "potter." How far psychical terms like "knowledge" or "love" can be analogically applied beyond human application is an interesting question, but it seems clear that here, too, there is ample room (contra Taylor) for a defender of the ontological argument to nonetheless traverse quite a distance down the *via negativa*. No theist wants to say that God knows simply as a human being knows, hence Taylor needs to be more explicit regarding why we should believe that the ontological argument precludes defenders of it from *any* sort of belief in divine alterity. Of course merely absolute or nonrelative knowledge or love is a contradiction in terms in that a knower or lover presupposes an object known or a being who is loved, but what contradiction is there in claiming that God *exists* necessarily (i.e., absolutely without dependence on any particular others)?

Rather than an exalted Taylor-like negative theology, it makes sense, on Taylor's own grounds, to think through carefully apophatic or negative anthropology. Do we know with *complete* assurance anything? If to know something is to have conclusive, final evidence (admittedly, a questionable assumption), then perhaps only God knows:

I really believe that we know what "knowledge" is partly by knowing God, and that though it is true that we form the idea of divine knowledge by analogical extension from our experience of human knowledge, this is not the whole truth, the other side of the matter being that we form our idea of human knowledge by exploiting the intuition . . . which we have of God. To "know" *ought* to mean, having conclusive evidence, such as God has, shutting off the very possibility of error; but to apply this idea to man we must tone it down drastically indeed. . . . Man loves, but how far and how much? He either hates or is apathetic towards most of his surroundings. It is God who loves – without any distorting antipathies or blind spots of mere indifference. God loves the creatures – period.

We love a few creatures some of the time, and seldom or never wholly without complicating feelings of vanity, envy, irritation, fear, and the like. (Hartshorne 1970, 155–156)

That is, "human knowledge" is not merely a designation for an otherwise inaccessible divine nature, as Taylor indicates, in that it may also be a derivative concept.

The real problem, as Hartshorne sees things, correctly I think, is not that we would exaggerate the degree to which we could accurately describe God, but rather that we would engage in a sort of idolatry of divine being, cause, and absoluteness as substitutes for divine being-becoming, cause-effect, absoluteness-relativity (or relationality).

Taylor's view seems to be that the word "God" refers to what is left when we deny all that we know: nothing. The importance of a positive conception of perfection is precisely that it enables us to avoid this conclusion. The praise that is given by deconstructionist a/theologians to the view that *all* of our knowledge is inaccurate, so we need to negate it so as to arrive at God, is misplaced if what we really arrive at as a result of this view is nonbeing. As Cleanthes argues in Hume's *Dialogues Concerning Natural Religion*, a negative theology that is too aggressive leads, quite simply, to atheism.

A defensible view of negation, by way of contrast, follows Plato's distinction in the *Sophist* (256–259) between absolute and relative nonbeing.

The former (as Parmenides and Bergson, among others, have realized) is unintelligible in that to think or say *it* is no longer to think or say absolutely nothing, but something. To legitimately say that something is nothing is to say that it is nothing like some other thing. That is, relative nonbeing is a synonym for otherness such that every negation implies an affirmation. As a result, to say that "God does not exist" implies something positive about reality that makes this statement true. Usually it is the reality of evil in the world that is assumed to provide the evidence in that evil is assumed to be incompatible with the existence of an omnipotent and omniscient (with respect to future contingencies) God. As is well known, however, in Hartshorne's process or neoclassical theism these attributes are reconsidered such that evil need not have the negating power that atheists or deconstructionists assume it has (Hartshorne 1984b).

The problem with atheism here is that it is surprisingly too "a prioris- tic." It *assumes* that God must have the traditional attributes, then notices evil in the world that is inconsistent with these attributes, which leads to a rejection of belief in God. It is better to start more empirically by noticing evil in the world (as the Greeks realized, life is tragic) and then try to figure out what sort of God, if any, would be compatible with such a world. That is, a defense of the ontological argument is obviously an exercise in a priori reasoning, but this exercise in conceptual clarification of the concept of perfection can easily be part of a more extensive philo- sophical effort that includes empirical and phenomenological features. Reflective equilibrium is reached when all of these features are in balance with each other. Further, it should be noted that by a priori I obviously do not mean a type of reasoning that is prior to all experience (this would be impossible), but rather a type of reasoning that is compatible with any experience and is independent of any particular, contingent aspect of experience.

The important thing when developing a defensible view of negation is to avoid both the treatment of absolute nonbeing as an agent and the assumption that one can talk sense about "it." Heidegger seems to do precisely this, with Taylor in his wake, when he famously (or infamously) uses the phrase *"Das nichts nichtet."* Perhaps the best way to translate this phrase is by saying that "The activity of nothing simply consists in nothing" or "The nothing is nothing." But, quite frankly, I am at a loss regarding whether or not it is an unfair, yet humorous, typical Anglo-American car- icature of Heidegger (and, by implication, of Taylor) or a more accurate scholarly translation to render this phrase in English as "The nothing noths." Such a treatment of absolute nonbeing as having agency seems, in context, to be implied in Heidegger's version of a legitimate metaphysical question, "Why is there something rather than [absolutely] nothing?" (Heidegger 1959, 19; cf. Hare 1981).

In the *Sophist* (247) Plato makes it clear that *anything* has being if it exhibits the dynamic power (*dynamis*) to affect others, or to be affected by them, in however slight a way. On this instructive definition, Heidegger's (and presumably Taylor's) nothingness that "noths" is really something. "The being of total nonbeing, the falsity of all possible assertions, is a [needless] paradox" created when language is idling. Rather than ask the Heideggerian question, it makes more sense to ask, "Since there must be something (absolute nonbeing lacking coherent meaning) . . . what is the necessary content of the something in distinction from the contingent entities that may or may not be?" (Hartshorne 1983, 328). Or again:

An all too negative theology made God the great emptiness, and an all too negative anthropology made the creatures also empty. I suggest that nothing is only nothing, that the divine attributes are positive, and the creatures' qualities are between these and nothing. (Hartshorne 1962, 147; also 1948, 34–36)

If God is related sympathetically to others in a categorically unique way (in that we relate to others only intermittently and in attenuated fashion, whereas the greatest conceivable being-in-becoming would do so always and with ideal intensity), then rather than say that the divine actuality is nonrelative we should say that it is superrelative. If a negative theologian is *thinking of God* he or she is doing something more than merely refusing to apply human concepts to deity. He or she must in *some* sense be applying human concepts to deity. The contention of the Hartshornian, process, neoclassical theist is that we have reason to apply absoluteness (nonrelativity) to divine *existence* as a result of the ontological argument. This is not only compatible with, but actually requires, an omnitemporal relativity in the divine *actuality*. God is supergood (rather than nongood) in the sense that, as the greatest conceivable being-in-becoming, God's supreme love would require others with whom to be related in a loving way.

In short, the traditional *via negativa* both presupposed (albeit confusedly so) the *via positiva* and was victim of a monopolar prejudice wherein one column of divine attributes (being, absoluteness, etc.) was privileged at the expense of a correlative column of attributes (becoming, relativity, etc.). If God was allowed to be more absolute than absoluteness as humanly conceived, why not also say that God is more related to others (i.e., is more relative with respect to others) than relativity as humanly conceived? The deconstructionist *via negativa,* by way of partial contrast, both tries in vain, as far as I can tell, to extricate itself altogether from the *via positiva* and relies for its best insights on criticizing the many silly things said by traditional theists over the centuries. We can do better, I think, than either traditional or deconstructionist apophatic theology (or a/theology).

Once again, if the ontological argument fails, it is not due to anything that Taylor says; as a result, reports of the nonviability of philosophy may very well be, as we have seen, like reports of Mark Twain's death and the death of the ontological argument, premature.

The Hegelian Background

In order to be fair to Taylor and to better understand, by way of partial contrast, the neoclassical use of the ontological argument, it will profit us to more carefully consider the ways in which Taylor's examination of the ontological argument relies heavily on Hegel's (not Hartshorne's, Malcolm's, or Findlay's) version of it.

Taylor thinks, along with Tillich (Tillich 1964, 10), that the ontological argument is an effort to overcome estrangement from God, whereas the cosmological argument is an intellectual effort that results in our meeting a divine stranger. But the two arguments are not on a par in that the ontological argument is presupposed by the cosmological argument. Indeed it is presupposed by *any* intellectual activity, on the Hegelian view that Taylor takes as his starting point. Taylor may be correct in noting that if this claim is hyperbolic, it is a type of exaggeration that is only possible in the rationalist tradition of Descartes, Leibniz, and Spinoza, rather than in the empiricist tradition of Collins, Toland, and Paley. These latter thinkers all offered versions of the cosmological or teleological arguments, whereas the rationalist thinkers all offered versions of the ontological argument (Taylor 1977, 211–212).

As a result of the religious skepticism of Hume's posthumous *Dialogues Concerning Natural Religion* and Kant's first critique, it seemed that, regarding arguments for the existence of God, two options remained open: Humean agnosticism or Kantian fideism. Taylor's admiration for Hegel seems to be due in part to the latter's negotiation around this impasse. Specifically, Hegel's *Lectures on the Philosophy of Religion* result in one long, complex *argument* for God's existence. Taylor unfortunately says "proof" for God's existence, which is a bit too strong. By expecting too much from theistic metaphysics at the outset (the essay in question

comes from early in Taylor's career), one can make it too easy to later
urge its deficiencies (Taylor 1977, 212).

On Taylor's reading of Hegel, the cosmological and teleological arguments start from experience in the world and argue for God as the ground
or cause of such experience. By way of contrast, the ontological argument
begins with the concept of God "and tries to establish God's being *and
the actuality of the world*" (Taylor 1977, 213 – emphasis added). Although
Hegel is insightful in bringing these three arguments for the existence
of God together in what Hartshorne calls one "global" argument, he
overstates the results of the ontological argument when he alleges that
through it we can know not only *that* God exists necessarily, but also
how God exists concretely from moment to moment – indeed, how the
world exists from moment to moment! This breathtaking ambition for
the ontological argument is something of an embarrassment for many of
its defenders, who think that it is not a small accomplishment to learn
that God exists without the possibility of nonexistence. What more could
one want from a single argument?

Further, Taylor, following Hegel, in a related move, seems too quick to
identify God with the infinite. The ontological argument does reach the
conclusion that God is infinite *in existence*, but if the greatest conceivable
being has real relations with finite creatures through knowledge and love,
God would in some (positive) sense be finite, too. This is an insight that
Hegel himself, or Taylor on Hegelian grounds, should have reached,
given their belief that the contingent and the necessary, the finite and
the infinite, respectively, are not so much contradictories as they are
correlative opposites (Taylor 1977, 213–214, 218).

I would like to return to the idea, shared by Hegel and Hartshorne,
that the three arguments (cosmological, teleological, and ontological)
are parts of one complex or global argument. Whereas each of these
arguments offers for Hartshorne a different *angle* on God's existence, for
Hegel they correlate, as we have seen, with different *stages* of the philosophy of religion: the cosmological with the religion of nature, the teleological with the religion of spiritual individualism, and the ontological
with "absolute religion." These first two stages are not so much negated
as they are sublated or preserved in the march toward the ontological argument. Or again, the first two arguments constitute Hegel's St.
Bonaventure-like *Itinerarium Mentis in Deum*, the mind's road to God,
whereas the ontological argument involves the *Descensus Dei in Mundum*,
the divine descent back to the world so as to overcome estrangement
between the divine and the human, as mentioned above regarding

Tillich. Thus, as in Kant, the cosmological and teleological arguments presuppose the ontological one in that these upward and downward movements are but moments in one overall argument (Taylor 1977, 215–216).

But the ontological argument is the most complete of the three in that it more fully contains the other two, on Hegel's and Taylor's view. The cosmological and teleological arguments enable us to have a concept of God that is, despite Taylor's apophatic worries, at least adequate enough to get the ontological argument moving. So far, so good. However, we have seen that problems arise when Taylor follows Hegel in suggesting that the ontological argument advances "from the pure notion to its concrete existence" (Taylor 1977, 224). The word "concrete" is problematic here because it gives the impression that the ontological argument is meant not only to show the rationality of believing in the necessary existence of God, but also to deduce something from an abstract concept regarding *how* God exists from moment to moment and regarding the concrete details of other existents.

Further, Hegel is not always clear that it is the concept of the greatest conceivable being or the concept of perfection in particular that leads to the conclusion regarding necessary existence. Likewise, Taylor sometimes follows Hegel in giving the impression that it is thought in general that is in dialectical unity with being or existence. Language regarding the identity of pure thought and pure being in both Hegel and Taylor is likely to leave at least some readers scratching their heads and hence should perhaps be dropped in any effort to make the ontological argument understandable to contemporary readers. Likewise, it would be best to leave aside Hegel's distinctly Christian version of the argument wherein the rational meaning of the ontological argument is realized most fully in the incarnation of the divine *logos* (Taylor 1977, 225, 227, 230). One of the virtues of the ontological argument is that it is cast at such a high level of abstraction that it can be found appealing by scholars in several quite different religious traditions.

My purpose here is not the typical Hegel-bashing that goes on among English-language philosophers. Despite the fact that certain phrases used in Hegel's and Taylor's treatments of the ontological argument sound odd – as in "the reunion of subjectivity and objectivity" – there is much to be gained from Hegel's effort to show how the cosmological, teleological, and ontological arguments are linked in one overall rational argument for the existence of God. Specifically, the former two arguments help us to develop the concept of God that gets the ontological argument started. The stumbling block that keeps coming up both in Hegel's *Lectures on the*

Philosophy of Religion and in Taylor's treatment of Hegel is the very obstacle that leads agnostics like Oppy to reject the ontological argument. Hegel and Taylor give the impression to agnostics like Oppy that one is moving in the ontological argument from a mere notion to *actuality*. This is where Hartshorne's contribution to the ontological argument is unfortunately not as well known as it should be: in the ontological argument one need not (as Hegel, Taylor, and Oppy assume) move from concept to actuality (Taylor 1977, 229) in that such a move is, as Oppy correctly urges, a category mistake. Rather, one need only move from a certain concept (of perfection) to the inference that God's *existence* is necessary; no inference need be made, nor can one legitimately be made, to divine or other *actuality*.

To put the point in Heideggerian terms that might be appealing to Taylor, the ontological argument concerns not any particular facts about God, but what it is to be a fact; it concerns the category of fact, rather than any particular application of this category; it indeed concerns the ontological rather than the ontic.

Taylor's A/theology

Taylor's ultimate aim regarding the ontological argument, it seems, is to suggest that it is worthless. In this regard he is, strange as this sounds, much like the analytic philosopher Graham Oppy. It is not insignificant that the version of the ontological argument that he chooses to criticize is Hegel's. Despite Hegel's commendable effort to link the ontological with the cosmological and teleological approaches, so that each of these three is a part of one global argument, he exhibits a glaring weakness: the effort to infer knowledge of concrete actuality (whether divine or human) from an abstract concept. By focusing on this weakness, Taylor has a convenient (too convenient!) target for his own misology. A direct hit is expected and not surprisingly delivered (Taylor 1999a, 33–34).

Taylor admires Nietzsche as one of the prophets of postmodernism. When he famously (or infamously) said, relying on Hegel, that God is dead, he was summarizing the results that were in the making at least since the time of Hume and Kant. Reformulations of theism, in general (including Whitehead's and Hartshorne's), and of the ontological argument, in particular, do not go far enough, on Taylor's view, to deconstruct theism. Process theism, in general, and the ontological argument, in particular, exhibit too much confidence in rationality. Such confidence should have ended with Hegel, as Taylor sees things (Taylor 1984, 3–5,

30–31, 37, 66, 98, 119, 134–135; Kung 1980, 138–142). This is why it is important to highlight versions of the ontological argument that rely on a less hubristic, more fallibilist, view of rationality than Hegel's.

The death of God also signifies for Taylor the death of the traditional regime of rationality in that an omniscient God, if such exists, becomes the standard of knowledge (Taylor 1997, 232–233). To put the point in Heideggerian terms that are presumably acceptable to Taylor, the dominant philosophical tradition in the West is "ontotheological." This ontotheological economy (in the sense of managing the household of philosophy) is at once religious and epistemological. Taylor is surely correct to commend Thomas Altizer in his criticism of the transcendence of the God of classical theism, an Unmoved Mover who can be seen as immanent in the world, or to have knowledge of it or to care for it, only at the price of consistency. This inconsistency is especially odd in an incarnational religion like Christianity (Taylor 1990, 15, 76; Altizer 1977).

Alleged problems with the identification of an omniscient God and truth take us to the heart of Taylor's view of the ontological argument. In fact, this argument does not really concern the existence of God, as he sees things (relying on Tillich), but rather functions primarily to supply the collateral for humanity's loan on truth. Rational efforts to get at the truth presuppose God as omniscient; if God cannot be thought not to exist (as in the ontological argument), then the truth cannot be thought not to exist. But truth, on Taylor's view, which is at once deconstructionist and social constructionist, does not really exist (Taylor 1990, 82–83; Tillich 1964). It seems that, as a consequence of the Nietzsche-like and/or Altizer-like death of God that fascinates him, Taylor should be driven toward atheism or agnosticism. But he seems instead to move toward an oxymoronic affirmation of the hiddenness of God; toward the paradoxical kataphatic declaration of apophaticism (Taylor 1992, 155).

How are we to account for Taylor's affirmation here and for this tentative kataphaticism? He has no rational case for the existence of God to rely on. Are his affirmative statements and his flirtations with kataphaticism expressions of a Kierkegaardian fideism? If so, he is open to the familiar challenge of Schopenhauer: if the religious believer relies entirely on faith and not reason for the affirmation that God exists, why cannot the agnostic or atheist just as easily declare a lack of faith? A more defensible theism, it seems, would acknowledge a debt to St. Anselm and to other sophisticated defenders of the fallibilist rationality of religious belief, as in Peirce (cf. Taylor 1999a, 23, 153).

Taylor is adamant that his a/theology is not to be identified with atheism, but with a "nonnegative negative theology." (I assume that the two
negatives in the first word signify some sort of kataphatic positive.) In
this view one discerns the unsaid in the midst of the said such that the
apophatic is but one deconstructionist moment in ongoing theological
process. Once again, this is fine as far as it goes. But how to account in
Taylor for the other, kataphatic moment (Taylor 1999a, 40)?

In opposing the ontotheological tradition, along with Heidegger,
Taylor is militating against metaphysical thinking that has often included
appeal to the ontological argument. He seems to think that metaphysics
necessarily encourages the annihilation of, or escape from, time, as in
Aristotelian unmoved movers or the Boethian *totum simul*, both of which
have admittedly had an enormous influence on the history of metaphysics. But Taylor does not engage here the major figures in process
metaphysics, who are firmly committed to the reality of time: Peirce,
Bergson, Whitehead, and Hartshorne. Metaphysical realities are *not* those
that escape from time, but are those that are instantiated in every moment
of time. They endure everlastingly. Likewise, *some* theists emphasize divine
unity to the exclusion of multiplicity or diversity, but not all, as Taylor
implies. Neoclassical or process theists admit the plurality of divine states,
a multiplicity of contingent experiences as God actualizes from moment
to moment the divine necessary existence (Taylor 1987, xxvi, 66, 188,
198, 256).

Thus, Taylor is premature in dismissing metaphysics in general along
the lines of a Heideggerian critique of the metaphysics of presence. If
ontotheology is seen as presupposing a metaphysics of presence, wherein
"presence is undisturbed by absence," then it would make sense for
Taylor to engage more directly the religious language used by a defender
of the ontological argument like Hartshorne. In the latter's religious
language, as we have seen, only the most abstract divine attributes can
be discussed literally; the other attributes can only be discussed in analogical or symbolic terms, leaving much elbow room for divine "absence."
How God exists from moment to moment in the divine actuality is *not*
present to us, even if we have a sound version of the ontological argument in place. Further, an everlasting God would not so much privilege
the temporal modality of the present, as Taylor seems to fear, in that the
greatest conceivable being would have existed in every past moment and
would remember such; and will exist in every future moment and ideally
anticipates such to the extent possible (Taylor 1999b, 66–70).

Rorty, Again

Before moving to the remaining chapters of the book, which deal with four analytic philosophers who have recently written on the ontological argument, it will be profitable to try to consolidate the efforts of the present chapter and the previous one, both of which have dealt with thinkers heavily influenced by deconstructionism.

In their more radical moments, Rorty and Taylor give their readers the impression that they regard all intellectual discourse as play or fantasy, thus aligning themselves with Derrida. And like Derrida they are, as George Shields rightly argues, vulnerable regarding their at least apparent rejection of standard canons of critical thinking and standard logical principles (Shields 2003, 45–46). For example, Derrida speaks (in response to Searle) of a "tone of aggrievement" when he is misinterpreted, despite the fact that he has no "position" or "argument" to be misinterpreted (see Ellis 1989). Of course the charge of misology against Derrida, Rorty, and Taylor will receive the following rejoinder: these thinkers are not opposed to logic, rather they are using an "other" (in Taylor's case, apophatic) logic. I have argued, however, that Rorty and Taylor have not provided sufficient evidence, in addition to their impressive rhetoric, regarding how this new rationality or new logic would work in practice. For example, both thinkers presuppose the very principle of noncontradiction that they seem to call into question, as when Rorty wonders why philosophers came to think that logic (including its key principle regarding noncontradiction) was sublime.

I hope that I have also made it clear that there are some things for which Rorty and Taylor should be commended. It is true, for example, that linguistic meanings are sometimes unstable, although Rorty and Taylor hyperbolize when they indicate that this tendency is pervasive of all discourse (Shields 2003, 46). Likewise, there is much to be said in favor of apophaticism, as defenders of the ontological argument have admitted from the time of St. Anselm to the present. In Chs. 16–17 of *Proslogion*, Anselm, echoing Plato, compares God to an unapproachable light like the sun, a hiddenness that *in a sense* makes God ineffable. But this use of negative theology does not get in the way of his contention that the divine nonexistence is inconceivable. As Hartshorne puts the point, what Anselm shows (contra Rorty and Taylor) is that:

God's reality must be more than . . . necessary existence, and must include a wealth of positive and contingent qualities or aspects. An analogy: each moment of my personal existence is concretized anew, but just how, in just what experiences, is always an additional fact, not deducible from the bare truth that I continue existing. Moreover, my individuality might not have been, and I might soon not be, concretized in any way at all. The divine individuality, by contrast, has this unique superiority: it must always be and have been concretized somehow. Only the *how*, not the *that*, is here contingent. (see Hartshorne's "Introduction" to Anselm 1982, 17)

That is, even if there is a legitimate place for the negative way in the work of those who defend the ontological argument, "God is not fundamentally negative" (Hartshorne 1941, 323).

In Taylor's case, at least, if not in Rorty's, the lack of clarity regarding the relationship between the kataphatic and the apophatic can be traced back to a lack of clarity in Hegel's use of the ontological argument. The neoclassical view may be right or wrong, but it is at least clear:

God is not in every sense self-sufficient, for although He exists independently, He depends for His particular actuality, on *how* he exists, upon what other things exist. Necessary or absolute in His bare essence and existence as divine, or simply as God, He is yet, in His concrete actuality, contingent, relative, and forever incomplete, because forever in process of further enrichment, value possibilities being inexhaustible. This, roughly stated, is neoclassical theism. (Hartshorne 1965, 235 – once again, late in his career Hartshorne dropped male pronouns when talking of either God or human beings)

Hegel's view of the same subject matter is quite unclear, however. This view is, according to Hartshorne, "a perpetual, systematic muddle between classical theism, classical pantheism, and something like neoclassical theism, with a dose of humanistic atheism, or the self-deification of man, thrown in for good measure" (Hartshorne 1965, 235). It is doubtful if even a sympathetic interpreter of Hegel (e.g., Desmond 2003), and a fortiori of Taylor, can clarify the relationship between what can and cannot be said regarding God.

4

Is the Ontological Argument Worthless?

Graham Oppy's Rejection

Epistemological Conservativism

In order to orient ourselves with respect to Graham Oppy's encyclopedic and scholarly study of the ontological argument, it will be helpful to point out conflicting evidence in his book regarding two key issues. The first concerns the extent to which, and the ways in which, Oppy rejects the argument. In this regard it is important to emphasize that he remains throughout an agnostic, rather than an atheist. And the second concerns a key premise in the ontological argument that alleges that we can, in fact, have a clear enough concept of the greatest conceivable being to get the argument started.

Oppy starts from an epistemological assumption that he shares with some religious believers. This is the tenet that is crucial to reformed epistemology, that philosophical views should be presumed innocent until convicted. This gives elbow room for theists, atheists, and agnostics alike to hold their respective views. Like Oppy, it is probable that each one of us has friends in each of these camps and it would be obnoxious to claim that everyone outside of one's own camp is irrational. The initial solace provided to the defender of the ontological argument by this stance is erased, however, when Oppy claims that there is nothing in the ontological argument that could bring a reasonable agnostic around to an acceptance of this argument (Oppy 1995, xiii, 330).

At other points in his book Oppy thinks of himself as offering a *refutation* of the ontological argument, which is a much more ambitious task than merely stating that defenders of the ontological argument are not likely to dislodge agnostics like himself from their views. In fairness to

Oppy it should be noted that throughout his book he thinks that theists can legitimately use the ontological argument in the *exposition* of their view, but such a use is, he thinks, *dialectically inefficacious*. Putting these two ambitions together – one modest and the other bold in the Popperian sense – it seems that we can, when aided by an application of the principle of charity, derive the following conclusion: according to Oppy, the ontological argument helps to make theistic epistemology secure, but it does not show that nontheism is unintelligible or indefensible. That is, theism may be epistemically secure, but it is not absolutely secure (Oppy 1995, xviii, 186).

Some theists, those influenced by reformed epistemology, seem to agree with Oppy in this conclusion (e.g., Plantinga 1974). The ontological argument, he alleges, shows that it is rational to *accept* theism, but not that one can *prove* it. Or again, the ontological argument shows that it is reasonable to accept the conclusion *if* the premises to the argument are reasonable, but the ontological argument itself does not, he argues, establish the reasonableness of the premises (Oppy 1995, 187–189; also 1992a; 1992b; Oppy, Jackson, and Smith 1994; and Oppy and O'Leary-Hawthorne 1997).

Which premises?, it might be asked. We have seen that the most questionable premise, on Hartshorne's reasoning, is that which states that we *can* conceive of God as the greatest conceivable being. Surprisingly, Oppy seems to concede that he can "perfectly well understand" this premise (Oppy 1995, 194, 332). (It is unclear, however, what Oppy means by saying that the coherence of the concept of God is a "factual matter" – Oppy 1995, 293.) This concession, along with his affinity with reformed epistemology or epistemological conservativism, distinguishes Oppy's agnosticism from, say, Salmon's atheism, wherein the hypothesis of God's existence is "fundamentally implausible" (Salmon 1987, 101).

I would like to emphasize, in agreement with Thomas Schmidt, that there is much to be said in favor of reformed epistemology in a *political* context. As long as the rights of others are not being violated, people should be free to believe what they want to believe or feel compelled to believe. The innocent until convicted slogan works well here. It is only when one tries to restrict the liberty of others as a result of one's beliefs that one is bound to give reasons for one's beliefs in a situation of intersubjective, mutual respect (Schmidt forthcoming). In a *metaphysical* context, however, we want intersubjective rationality at work from the outset in that metaphysics, unlike politics, is a rational discipline through and through.

Although Oppy admits that he can conceive of a "most perfect being" or a "maximally great being," he is not *required* to do so. (One is tempted to say: of course not!) Further, he thinks that any version of the ontological argument that is remotely plausible can also, from a different point of view, be parodied along the lines of Gaunilo's famous *reductio*. As before, the ontological argument is, according to Oppy, dialectically impotent in the effort to change the minds of agnostics. It is for this reason that Oppy sees it as "completely worthless" and that his verdict concerning it is "entirely negative" (Oppy 1995, 199). Thus, we can see that Oppy's cherished view seems to be not the mild one to the effect that the ontological argument is innocent until proven guilty; his critical verdict regarding this argument is, once again, *entirely* negative. It is *completely* worthless, he thinks.

Although Oppy frequently mentions Hartshorne's defense of the ontological argument, he gives no evidence whatsoever that he is familiar with Hartshorne's neoclassical use of the argument. When he wonders if there could possibly be a greatest being in light of the fact that our knowledge is always unfinished, always changing, he has an excellent opportunity to introduce his criticisms of neoclassical theism, but this opportunity is missed. That is, when Oppy refers to God he refers to the God of classical theism (e.g., Oppy 1992c). This is unfortunate because of the distinct advantage involved in the neoclassical distinction between divine existence and divine actuality: the ontological argument need not be seen as moving from an abstract concept to concrete reality, but rather it moves from an abstract concept to the abstract conclusion that God must necessarily exist in *some* concrete state or other, where the precise character of these concrete states is determined by contingent events as they come into existence from moment to moment. Oppy does agree with Hartshorne, however, as we saw in Oppy's assessment of Hume, that it is question-begging to *assume* that anything that exists does so contingently. The whole point to the ontological argument is to establish the necessary existence of a perfect being (Oppy 1995, 295, 297).

Oppy thinks of himself as offering a moderate stance in that he is opposed not only to the Humean assumption that all existence *has to be* contingent, but also to overly aggressive uses of the ontological argument, to uses of the argument that try to *prove* the existence of God rather than to explicate why it makes sense on epistemologically conservative grounds to believe in God. For example, the insistence that belief in God is required once one possesses the concept of God is a piece of "linguistic imperialism" or "logomachy" (Oppy 1995, 202, 335).

Oppy would be on safer ground, however, if he denied that we can have an adequate concept of God. That is, both Hartshorne's and my own defenses of the ontological argument are hardly imperialistic in that they involve hypothetical reasoning (cf. Plato's anticipation of the ontological argument, which moves beyond hypotheses): *if* we can get a coherent concept of the greatest being, of God, then we can know that this being exists necessarily.

One of the dangers posed by epistemological conservativism is that a sort of evidentiary Balkanization could occur, wherein each group would stick to its own kind of reasoning with little or no adjudication of disputes occurring among groups. This danger is brought to the fore by Mark Nelson, who argues that the best judges of arguments for the existence of God are those theists whose belief in God is properly basic; that is, theists who do not take the rationality of their belief to depend on any theistic argument (Nelson 1996).

Oppy is correct to try to avoid this danger: "It is far from obvious that there is any sense of 'expertise' in which moderately intelligent persons ought to feel the need to defer to 'expert' opinion when confronted with questions about the convincingness of *any* arguments for the existence of God" (Oppy 1998, 35). Although he was not an epistemological conservative, some contemporary theists might point to Norman Malcolm as someone offering such an expert opinion. But Oppy asks (derisively, I think, and without argument), "Who would not now be embarrassed to have been a proponent of Malcolm's version of the ontological argument in *Proslogion* 3?" (Oppy 1998, 37). Despite his unjustified disparagement of Malcolm (and presumably of other defenders of the ontological argument), Oppy's general point here seems on the mark:

> ...we try to make sure that partisan desires play no part in judicial decisions. In the philosophical case, those of us who are not inclined to follow James' line on the will to believe may well feel that it is an individual failing to allow desires to infect our judgments about the worth of arguments – but we are not likely to follow Clifford in holding that those who do allow desire to infect judgment in this way somehow pollute the intellectual environment for everyone else. (Oppy 1998, 37)

In the philosophical case we acknowledge that desire-independence is an ideal to which we aspire, even if Oppy thinks that we do not need to build in provisions (as in the legal case) to prevent desire-dependence from entering our decisions where we need to be as objective as possible. It should be noted, however, that Rawls' veil of ignorance is precisely such a provision in a philosophical, rather than in a legal, context. There is no need, Oppy rightly admits, to run to the other extreme from Nelson and have nontheists be privileged judges regarding, say, the ontological argument (Oppy 1998, 38–43).

On the analogy once again of legal reasoning, the important thing is to be fair. But we have seen that Oppy wavers in his attempt to be as fair as possible. At times he characterizes his view as "weak agnosticism" and at other times as "fallibilist atheism." The latter seems to be a much stronger rejection of theism than the former: atheism is made the default position unless the ontological or some other argument comes along to topple it. It is unlikely this will occur, he thinks (Oppy 1994, 147).

Oppy's preferred view, however, seems to be weak agnosticism. Two sorts of agnosticism are distinguished. Strong agnosticism holds that it is *obligatory* to suspend judgment regarding God's existence, whereas in weak agnosticism it is *permissible* for reasonable people to suspend judgment regarding God's existence. Strong agnosticism emphasizes the claim that the lack of evidence for the existence of God is crucial, whereas weak agnosticism is built on the principle that one may continue to believe in any view regarding the existence of God until one is given persuasive reasons not to do so.

It is clear in Oppy's debate with the strong agnostic that he is assuming that God has the attributes defended by classical theists, including a belief in God as an omnipotent creator of the universe *ex nihilo*. This is a significant assumption in that it leads him to doubt (contra evidence elsewhere in Oppy) if we can have a coherent concept of God, especially when the divine attributes are tested against the reality of evil in the world. Rather than considering the theodicy of neoclassical theists (e.g., Griffin 1976; 1991), wherein divine omnipotence is rethought, he assumes that the most likely theistic alternatives to classical theistic theodicy are: (a) polytheism, as in the famous consideration of malevolent deities in Hume's *Dialogues*; or (b) a theism that involves the denial of divine omnibenevolence, as in Jung. That is, Oppy's truncated conception of the theistic alternatives to classical theism makes it too easy for him to criticize monotheism, in general, and the ontological argument, in particular, in that these are assumed to be identical to their classical theistic versions (Oppy 1994, 148–149, 152).

It is to his credit, however, that Oppy points out some of the difficulties with strong agnosticism, which involves commitment to the implausible claim that belief in God is not rational. It is precisely such implausibility that usually leads Oppy (when he is not tempted by fallibilist atheism) to epistemological conservativism: the ontological argument shows, at the very least, that it is not irrational to believe in God. There is *some* affinity between Oppy and the strong agnostic, however. Both believe that we should concentrate our efforts on problems that are far more tractable than the existence of God, most notably problems associated with one's conduct in the *present* life (Oppy 1994, 151–152). Once again, Oppy's attenuated sense of the theistic alternatives to classical theism is in evidence in that Hartshorne, for example, is both a defender of the ontological argument *and* a critic of personal immortality (Dombrowski 2004, Ch. 10). His sort of theism, at least, is not open to the charge that it ignores the present life.

Oppy's tendency to engage in hyperbole makes for exciting reading, as when he says that there "is not the slightest evidence" that belief in God is rationally required (Oppy 1994, 157). He is *almost* correct in this regard. Anselm's discovery, it will be remembered, was that contingent existence is not compatible with perfection, hence God's existence is either impossible or necessary. Thus, unless one can show that the existence of God is logically impossible (or more loosely, that one cannot have a coherent concept of God), one *is* rationally required to believe in God. The option that allows one to say that God may or may not exist is at odds with the logic of perfection. We have seen conflicting evidence from Oppy regarding whether or not one can have a coherent concept of God; as a result, the question regarding whether or not believing in God is rationally required is not quite an open and shut one, as the language "not the slightest evidence" suggests.

Granted, the theist should proceed with trepidation when considering whether we are rationally *required* to believe in God, just as religious skeptics should proceed with trepidation when considering fallibilist atheism or strong agnosticism. In this regard, Oppy is most believable when he calls himself a weak agnostic: "There is no good methodological precept which says that a rational person will have a definite opinion about everything" (Oppy 1994, 162).

Billy Joe Lucas enables us to see what is most objectionable in Oppy's fluctuating position. Two points should be emphasized. First, Oppy has as a major goal to prove that no ontological argument is sound. That is, Oppy aims to *refute* all versions of the ontological argument (Oppy 1995, xviii). In order to do this, however, Oppy questions certain premises in certain versions of the ontological argument by saying that they are "controversial" or are "not above suspicion," which is not quite a negation of the premises in question. As Lucas rightly puts the point, "the game is not worth playing on Oppy's terms" (Lucas 1997, 182). Consider, for example, the premise found in many versions of the ontological argument that a concept of God is at least possible. At times Oppy grants this premise, as we have seen, and at other times (e.g., Oppy 1995, 262) he incredibly claims that no atheist or agnostic would grant this premise, and this despite the fact that Bertrand Russell, among other religious skeptics, concedes precisely this possibility. In short, as Lucas sees things, "an enumeration of *possible* objections does not an *actual* cogent and conclusive refutation make" (Lucas 1997, 183).

Second, Lucas is also instructive, as was noted in the Introduction, regarding the difficulties involved in communication across intradisciplinary lines in philosophy. But such communication, although difficult, is nonetheless crucial in the effort to respond to important contemporary objections to the ontological argument. The present book is concerned with influential continental approaches to the ontological argument as well as influential analytic approaches to the same. Both these types of approach need to be put into dialogue with neoclassical or process approaches to the ontological argument as they are found in the works of Lucas himself, and of Hartshorne, Goodwin, Viney, Towne, and Shields. We have heard already the hollow sound made by criticism of the ontological argument, criticism offered by Oppy and others, to the effect that the argument illegitimately moves from abstract theory to concrete actuality. Nothing could be further from the truth, given the neoclassical or process distinction between existence and actuality. As before, the argument moves from abstract theory to the conclusion that God must necessarily exist in *some* concrete state or other from moment to moment. But the precise character of these successive concrete states cannot be determined by abstract argument alone; much depends on the contingent decisions made by the creatures.

One might suspect that Oppy's divergent claims might be explained away due to the fact that they are separated by many pages and by many complicated arguments in his big book. The book is legitimately big in that he wishes to get a reticulative grasp of everything that has been said regarding the argument. But Robert Oakes alerts us to divergent claims in close proximity to each other in Oppy's book, as when Oppy claims that it could be reasonable for some theists to hold that there are sound ontological arguments right before he claims that ontological arguments are completely worthless (Oppy 1995, 194, 199). One wonders along with Oakes: how could a completely worthless argument be believed by some rational parties to be sound (Oakes 1998, 382)?

We have seen that defenders of the ontological argument, assuming that they are intellectually honest and possess a certain degree of epistemological modesty, are willing to admit that the argument falls short of indubitable *proof* (in that the argument assumes that we can, in fact, have a sufficiently clear concept of God), and that the claim that one is rationally *required* to believe in God as a result of the ontological argument should be taken with several grains of salt. But to admit this much is not to claim, as Oppy mistakenly thinks, that the argument is dialectically impotent and worthless. As Oakes perceptively puts the point, to think that an argument is dialectically impotent and worthless because not all rational persons who are presented with the argument would accept it is to invite disaster for all philosophers: "by that austere a standard, of course, virtually all arguments with philosophically interesting conclusions – not just ontological arguments – would turn out to be 'worthless' " (Oakes 1998, 383).

Richard Gale indicates that the problems with Oppy's treatment of the ontological argument are noticed not only by philosophical theists, but also by religious skeptics like Gale himself. Unfortunately, Gale assumes that Oppy has offered dense and detailed expositions and criticisms of "every imaginable version" of the ontological argument, thereby indicating that he is no more aware of the neoclassical or process dimension of Hartshorne's version of the argument than Oppy. But Gale is nonetheless on the mark regarding Oppy's bottom-line assessment that all versions of the ontological argument are dialectically impotent and worthless. Gale thinks that this bottom-line assessment is "glib and shallow" (Gale 1998, 716). Gale's view here is noteworthy because he agrees with Oppy that ontological arguments typically move from an embedded premise in reference to God that becomes unembedded in the conclusion. A typical example is the transition from the premise that the *concept* of God (or the *definition* of God) involves existence to the conclusion that God exists. The fact that Gale says "exists" rather than "necessarily exists" seems to indicate that he has in mind the sort of argument found in Ch. 2 of Anselm's *Proslogion*, an argument that is inferior to the modal version found in Ch. 3, as we have seen. That is, what Gale seems to like in Oppy (the epistemological equivalence of the different versions of the ontological argument in *Proslogion* Chs. 2 and 3) needs historical analysis on Gale's part.

The point I wish to emphasize regarding Gale, however, is the extent to which he insightfully points out the weaknesses in Oppy's stance. We have seen the inconsistency in Oppy's wavering between the claim that all versions of the ontological argument are dialectically impotent and worthless, on the one hand, and the defense of a weak agnostic stance regarding the ontological argument, on the other. Gale helps us to examine more closely the latter stance in Oppy. Do we best capture this latter tendency in Oppy by saying that he is an agnostic or would we be better served, as Gale thinks, to refer to it as language-game fideism? Real agnostics, Gale argues, need not be committed to the sort of doxastic relativism practiced by Oppy when he is in his "agnostic" mode. Or again, to say, as Oppy does, that the theist can ignore the fact that there are reasonable agnostics and atheists or that agnostics can ignore the fact that there are reasonable theists and atheists (Oppy 1995, 197) is not exactly to offer a *defense* of agnosticism. Along the same lines, theists who profitably use the ontological argument, and hence who show that it is not worthless, *may* do so in defense of a Jamesian will to believe type of fideism, but more often they use it quite intelligibly as part of what John Haldane calls "faithful reason" (Haldane 2004).

When Oppy is not offering his "glib and shallow" opinion that the ontological argument is dialectically impotent and worthless, he offers a view that (unwittingly) *helps* a defender of the argument. This view has as its consequence:

...an epistemic tie or stalemate between the disputants, thereby meeting the epistemic undecidability condition for having a will-to-believe option. The most important, and disturbing, upshot of language-game fideism is that there is epistemic incommensurability between different doxastic practices. Second, the several different valid versions of the ontological argument, provided their controversial premises are logically independent of each other, could be agglomerated to establish the probability that God exists. (Gale 1998, 717)

This is surely welcome news to the philosophical theist, especially because it comes from a religious skeptic of Gale's stature. Although Gale is like Oppy in assuming that God must have all of the attributes found in classical theism, including omnipotence, he is nonetheless alert to the Balkanization of the dialectical context in philosophy of religion created by Oppy. People determine for themselves what is reasonable to believe, it seems, with little indication given regarding how those who disagree with each other are to relate (Gale 1998, 719).

The General Objection

Oppy's criticism of the ontological argument comes to a head in terms of what he calls "the general objection" to the argument. The objection is that defenders of the argument face a dilemma: either the argument is invalid, or, if it is valid, it depends on a premise that can be reasonably rejected. This objection applies to *all* versions of the ontological argument, he urges, in that they all rely on single terms and quantifiers used in the premises (names, definite descriptions like "the greatest conceivable being," indefinite descriptions like "a being than which none greater can be conceived," definitions, etc.); these are either embedded in the scope of further sentential operators or they are not so embedded; if they are not so embedded, an opponent to the argument can legitimately claim, he thinks, that the question of God's existence has been begged; however, if they are so embedded, it is illegitimate to detach the conclusion from the scope of these operators. We have seen in reference to Gale's critique that one way to put the general objection is to say that one cannot engage in a transition from the premise that the *concept* of God (or the *definition* of God) involves existence of some sort to the conclusion that God necessarily exists (Oppy 1995, 114–115; cf. Devine 1975c).

To be more precise, Oppy thinks that if these operators are extensional the question of God's necessary existence has been begged, whereas if they are intensional they do not require the desired conclusion. This enables us to see a bit more clearly why Oppy is (at least sometimes) willing to claim that agnostics and atheists *can* have a concept of God: to utter the words "God is a being than which no greater can be conceived" is to engage in a sort of role-playing comparable to saying that "Santa Claus lives at the North Pole." One is not thereby committing to a referent to the proper names used, hence the ontological argument *cannot be* dialectically effective. Only a "general endorsement of fallibilism" leads Oppy to soften his stance here (Oppy 1995, 116, 119).

One wonders, however, whether Oppy has really played the game. That is, role-playing and games can be quite serious (see, once again, the weighty implications of "playing the game" in Rawls' original position). If one can conjure in a clear way the concept of God, as Oppy sometimes admits (in contrast to many other agnostics or atheists), can one *really* conceive of such a being as nonexistent or as existing only contingently?

When faced with such a question, Oppy seems to retreat to what Hartshorne calls the "positivist" objection to the effect that we do not have an adequate concept of God as a being than which no greater can be conceived. Rather, this concept must be embedded within the scope of an operator. For example, Oppy would say that, according to the well-known view, God has certain properties. For some reason Oppy thinks that Hartshorne makes a concession to the religious skeptic at this point: either positivism (i.e., the view that we do not and cannot have an adequate concept of God) or the necessary existence of God is true and no a priori argument can force us to choose one way or the other. Indeed, this has always been Hartshorne's view (hence it is hardly a concession on his part) in that, although the ontological argument reaches the conclusion that God exists necessarily, the question as to whether we can have an adequate concept of God as a premise involves many contingencies (Oppy 1995, 280–281).

In addition to criticisms of Oppy's ambivalence regarding whether or not we can derive an adequate concept of God and regarding whether or not the ontological argument is necessarily impotent in dialectical contexts, other criticisms are possible. For example, Stephen Makin argues that because we can easily make sense of a concept that *cannot* be exemplified (an impossible being) we should also be able to make sense of a concept that *must be* exemplified (a necessary being). This is because all the modalities (impossibility, contingency, necessity) are interdefinable. Makin and Hartshorne disagree regarding the level of difficulty involved in citing an example of a necessarily exemplified concept (Makin thinks that the task is difficult, whereas Hartshorne thinks that "Something exists" is a rather straightforward implication of the realization that absolute nonexistence is unintelligible). But Makin nonetheless admits that there is no need to give a prior example of a necessarily exemplified concept for the ontological argument to go through. All that is needed is a "sufficiently well understood" concept of a being than which none greater can be conceived (Makin 1988, 83–84).

Oppy's response to Makin is hard to understand. He holds that "one can say that it is possible for a state of affairs to be necessary and yet for it not to be the case that that state of affairs actually occurs" (Oppy 1991, 107). A charitable interpretation of Oppy would be that his stance rests foursquare on a distinction between an extensional sense of conceptness and an intensional sense. In the former sense, X is a concept of something if and only if the extension of the concept is nonempty. In the latter sense, X is a concept of something if and only if X is a concept of a certain (intensionally) characterizable sort. That is, the extensional sense of a concept involves an external question, whereas the intensional sense of a concept does not.

In the quotation at the beginning of the previous paragraph, the first part of the sentence seems to refer to an intensional sense of conceptness and the second part to an extensional sense. Makin and other defenders of the ontological argument, Oppy thinks, equivocate on the sense of conceptness. If the extensional sense were used throughout, according to Oppy, we would beg the question regarding the necessary existence of God; but if the intensional sense were used throughout, the desired conclusion would not necessarily follow (although the desired conclusion is presumably a permissible one). The only way defenders of the ontological argument can make the argument work, he thinks, is by making an illicit move from an intensional concept as a premise to an extensional concept in the conclusion (Oppy 1991, 109–114; 1993a). This is his general objection to the ontological argument.

Makin initiates a telling response to Oppy that is dealt with in more detail by George Goodwin. If the question is asked, "What could there possibly be about a concept, beyond its coherence, that would necessitate its exemplification?," Makin responds by saying that there is something about one particular concept (something than which nothing greater can be conceived) that necessitates its exemplification. Necessity of exemplification is a source of greatness that is logically entailed by this particular concept (Makin 1992, 254; Wierenga 1998).

Bruce Langtry (Langtry 1999), like Makin, is skeptical of the claim that Oppy's general objection tears down all versions of the ontological argument. Although initially it seems that Oppy is willing to back down in light of Langtry's and Makin's objections, the retreat is only apparent in that he continues to think that a successful version of the ontological argument is "inconceivable" (Oppy 2001, 73, 79). One minor concession made is that the two alternatives, indeed a dilemma, offered in the general objection found in Oppy's book – that ontological arguments are either question-begging or invalid – are expanded into a trilemma. The third alternative is that the ontological argument might establish the existence of something uncontroversial, like the physical universe. Presumably this addition is an admission that, contra Hume, there *can* be necessary truths concerning existence, as in "Something exists."

The ontological argument is, in fact, strengthened by the conclusion that there can be necessary truths concerning existence. Further support for the argument comes from the conclusions to other theistic arguments, which, once again, reinforce each other like Peircian strands in a cable. For example, Charles Taliaferro points out that the argument from religious experience strengthens the claim (that is sometimes defended by Oppy and sometimes rejected) to the effect that we can have a concept of God. As Taliaferro insightfully puts the point: "it is... because of the interwoven nature of theistic arguments that establishing the 'complete worthlessness' of one is such a tall order" (Taliaferro 1997, 554).

De Re Modality

One crucial way to respond to Oppy's general objection is through a defense of the use of *de re* modality in the ontological argument. The best neoclassical efforts to mount such a defense have been made by George Goodwin and George Shields (see Shields 2003), and my intent here is to highlight and expand on their largely neglected efforts. As is well known, W. V. O. Quine and others have been critics of *de re* modality, whereas the possible worlds semantics argument of Saul Kripke and others has been used in its defense, as has the modal logic of Ruth Barcan. Oppy, it seems, leans in Quine's direction in this debate even if his view is not identical to Quine's (Oppy 1995, 143–152).

We should be clear at the outset that "a sound ontological argument will be a modal argument" (Goodwin 2003, 175). Further, the way or mode of existence is a property of every thing and every concept. Every existent thing exists either contingently or necessarily. Of course, no existent thing exists impossibly. In a similar way, any concept can be seen in one of three modes: either it must be instantiated in reality, or it might or might not be instantiated in reality, or it necessarily could not be instantiated in reality. "Necessity, contingency, impossibility: one of these three modalities of existence is a property of every being and every concept" (Goodwin 2003, 176).

Starting with this basis in modal logic, it can be said, minimally, that the ontological argument is not so much an unqualified proof that God exists, but rather that, of the three possible existential modalities, one is flat out incompatible with the concept of a perfect being. "Contingently existing perfect being" is just as contradictory as "round square." As we have seen, God's existence is either impossible or necessary. In effect, the ontological argument is a meta-argument: it is an argument about the logic of theistic arguments. Oppy does not really acknowledge, much less criticize, this point.

If the possibility of God's existence is evidence of God's necessary existence, the following argument can be developed:

1. Modality of existence is a predicate.
2. The existence of God is either necessary or impossible (due to the logic of perfection).

3. The existence of God is possible (conclusion from other theistic arguments, including the argument from religious experience).
4. The existence of God is necessary (from 1, 2, and 3 above) (based on Goodwin 2003, 176).

The first premise, which is in response to Kant's famous criticism, will be examined later. Assuming for the present that the first premise is acceptable, it looks like the most likely challenges to this argument are the positivist one and the modal objection. The positivist challenge, as we have seen, deals with the meaningfulness of the idea of divinity. The modal objection, however, challenges the assumption that there is a correspondence between logical or linguistic modalities (*de dictu*) and ontological or real modalities (*de re*).

The modal objection actually comes in two forms. One is the Kantian view that, although both logical modalities and ontological ones make sense, they do not correspond to each other, hence one cannot move in the same argument from logical necessity to ontological necessity. In effect, in this type of modal objection, the question of whether or not God exists is a function of something in addition to the coherence of our concepts; it is a function of the nature of reality. The other form of the modal objection, however, is more severe in that it claims that necessary ontological modality (i.e., *de re* modality) is nonsensical. As Goodwin sums the matter up: "These, then, are the three major challenges to a modal ontological argument: the positivistic challenge that the idea of God is nonsense, the Kantian challenge that the logical and ontological modalities are not coextensive, and the . . . objection that they could not be coextensive because ontological necessity is nonsensical" (Goodwin 2003, 177–178). A distinctive neoclassical theistic response to these two versions of the modal objection, which are variants of Oppy's general objection, comes by way of a metaphysics of temporal modality wherein the possible is defined in terms of the future. Further, by "the possible" I do not mean a radical difference between logical and real possibility.

I am defending the claim that God's existence is both logically necessary and ontologically necessary. There is no deviant conception of *de dictu* modality at work here in that it means the predication of a modal property to another proposition or dictum (hence *de dictu*). *De re* modality is also meant in a straightforward sense as the predication of a modal property to some real (hence *de re*) individual or thing. As a result of the ontological argument, to say that God *exists* necessarily is to say that God must be instantiated in *any logically possible world*. In this case logical and ontological modalities are coextensive.

It must be admitted that some have doubts that we could identify the same individual from world to world. One way to try to solve the problem of transworld identity is to isolate a thing's essence, in contrast to its accidental features. This sort of implicit Aristotelian essentialism is defective on the neoclassical view in that it implies that future stages of an individual's life already pre-exist, say in the mind of an omniscient God as classically conceived, who knows the individual's essence. But the future is not here yet to be known on the neoclassical view, not even by a divine being.

In neoclassical theism possible worlds are interpreted as *temporalistic*. It should be emphasized that possible worlds are not exotic places, like Thailand, but stipulated states of affairs. The question arises: what does it mean to say that a state of affairs is possible? Possibility is a relative term; that is, it is relative to the actual. Or again, "what is possible is what could be actual" (Goodwin 2003, 186). As I see things, both actuality and possibility involve time. To be precise, the actual is the past (what has already been actualized), the possible is the future (what has not yet been actualized), and the present is the current activity of becoming actual of what previously was possible.

The modal distinction in neoclassical theism is thus a temporal distinction. It is no longer possible that Mahler compose an opera; once it was possible that he do so. Hartshorne's way of putting the point is to say that although the present is internally related to the past, in that what exists in the present depends in some fashion on what has occurred in the past, the present is externally related to the future, which is not here yet as an actual influence. Not only are modal distinctions temporal; the converse is also true in that time is modal in structure. The past is modally different from the future: the past is cumulative, the region of what has been, whereas the future is indefinite, the region of what might be (Goodwin 2003, 196).

A further feature of this view is that logical possibility is not in theory different from real possibility: both must be compatible with actuality. A state of affairs that is "merely" logically possible usually means that the state of affairs is so far in the future that it seems practically irrelevant for present purposes. The key point is that logical possibilities, too, are temporally indexed: some states of affairs are *always* impossible (as in "round square") and some are *now impossible* but were *once possible*, as in Mahler's opera (Goodwin 2003, 187; Hartshorne 1963a).

The concept of necessity is a rich one on this temporalistic view. In addition to the distinction between *de re* and *de dictu* necessity, there is a distinction between conditional and unconditional necessity, leading to four types:

1. Conditional *de re* necessity.
2. Unconditional *de re* necessity.
3. Conditional *de dictu* necessity (truth in some, but not all, possible worlds).
4. Unconditional *de dictu* necessity (truth in every possible world) (based on Goodwin 2003, 188).

Goodwin's helpful example of (1) is the situation where, in every future in which human beings could exist, mortality is implied; however there are possible futures where human beings are excluded. In a similar way, "all humans are mortal" is an example of (3) in that it makes sense to say that "it is possible that there be no humans at some point in the future." The ontological argument is an attempt to show that God's existence is an example of (2). As Goodwin puts the point, "there is no future or once future state of affairs which excludes (or could exclude) the divine existence. Deity has the essential property of universal existential tolerance; it exists on any conditions whatsoever" (Goodwin 2003, 189). Likewise, "Necessarily, God exists" is an example of (4). In effect, (4) is parasitic on (2), not the other way around (also see Plantinga 1974, 28).

It should not escape our notice that: all four cases of necessity are defined in terms of possibility; possibility is defined in terms of the future; and *de dictu* necessity is defined in terms of *de re* necessity, rather than the other way around, as Oppy along with others supposes. The received view that seems to be accepted by Oppy is that necessity is to be defined in terms of analyticity, "but this is surely to guarantee by fiat that *de dictu* necessity will make sense and *de re* necessity will not" (Goodwin 2003, 189). It is *because* the necessary existence of God is a feature of all possible states of affairs (2) that the proposition affirming the necessity of God's existence (4) is itself necessary.

This neoclassical view is supported by the consideration that identifying an individual across possible worlds is not mysterious in the pejorative sense in that it is not much different from identifying an individual throughout time. This is due to the fact that possibility *is* futurity. On the substance metaphysics that Oppy and many others assume just is the view entailed by theism, the essential features of an individual are change-less and concrete. In the event metaphysics defended by neoclassical, process theists, however, changeless, concrete substances are not the ulti-mate metaphysical realities; rather, stable identities are abstractions from the final facts: occasions or events. That is, identity, even divine identity, is largely a retrospective abstraction. Essential properties or *de re* necessi-ties are the abstract features that will be instantiated in any future states. These *de re* necessities need be no more confusing than temporal modal-ities themselves (Goodwin 2003, 193).

One wonders why Oppy, in his detailed analysis of an amazing array of defenses of the ontological argument, does not deal with the neoclassical component of the argument in Hartshorne. Oppy, like Quine, seems to assume that transworld identity requires an Aristotelian essentialism that spans the different worlds. That is, he seems to assume *strict* identity rather than the *genetic* identity that is at work in neoclassical theism. In the former the identity is changeless and concrete, whereas in the latter the identity is changeless and abstract. As Goodwin once again intelligently puts the point regarding the similarity between transworld identity and identifying an individual through time: "Temporality is shown to be the interpretive key to *de re* modality. What is unintelligible is not *de re* necessity, but a substance interpretation of *de re* modality" (Goodwin 2003, 194; also Paulson 1984; Quine 1963).

These considerations bear directly on Oppy's general objection, which can be seen as a prohibition against moving from (embedded) abstract premises to a (unembedded) concrete conclusion. A concrete God can-not be derived from mere definitions and meaning postulates. The assumption seems to be that since concreteness involves contingency, the existence of a concrete God could never be analytically true. The confusion arises due to a misunderstanding concerning (or, better, an ignorance of) the relationship between the abstract and the concrete in the neoclassical concept of God. In this concept the abstract-concrete contrast is related to the existence-actuality contrast. God's *existence*, the fact *that* God exists, is an abstract constant; by way of contrast, God's *actu-ality*, or *how* God exists, is contingent and changes in concrete detail from moment to moment.

Although the abstract and the concrete are related in any individ-ual existing over time, the relationship between the two is asymmetri-cal (Goodwin 1983, 222). Dan-angry at some point in time presupposes Dan, but Dan does not presuppose Dan-angry. Likewise, divine existence requires *some* concrete manifestations, but which ones? Omnibenevolent ones, yes, but exactly which ones in concrete detail? Because the ontological argument need not conclude to any particular concrete divine states, it does not violate the widely held idea that concrete states are contingent. It must be admitted that in most cases existence as well as actuality is contingent, but there is nothing in the concept of existence itself that requires contingency. Thus, in the case of the greatest conceivable being one can conclude to the necessity of the divine existence, to "the necessary truth that there be some or other concrete divine states, but not any particular actual state" (Goodwin 1983, 224). Concrete existence is decidedly not derived from definitions or meaning postulates.

We have seen that possible worlds are not like distant planets, but are rather like counterfactuals or stipulated states of this world. If the world constantly changes, however, then possibility changes, too. That is, possibility is relative to the actual state of affairs; as the latter changes, so too the former: "What was possible may no longer be possible, and what is possible now may one day be impossible. In other words, possibility is inextricably linked to temporality" (Goodwin 1983, 226). On a phenomenological level we experience the future as a range of possibilities, with the limits of the range laid down by the past. Contingent (possible) truth might be false in some possible worlds, but necessary truth resists falsification in any possible world. Because God's existence is, as we have seen, an unconditional *de re* necessity, it would be illustrated at all times in every alternative future. Or more precisely, "if God exists, then God exists in all possible worlds; if God does not exist in all possible worlds, then God does not exist" (Goodwin 1983, 231).

Oppy's opposition to the ontological argument should be distinguished from those who are without qualification against the claim that logical possibility and metaphysical possibility are coextensive. Oppy admits that the differences between these two are not so clear and distinct that we can automatically reject the theistic idea that the logical possibility of God's existence is at the same time the metaphysical possibility of God's existence. That is, Oppy is aware of the fact that some opponents to the ontological argument are simply begging the question against their theistic opponents. To say that *de dictu* necessity and *de re* necessity are coextensive, however, is not to say that they are *identical* in that there is still the conceptual distinction between the two (Oppy 1995, 125–129).

It should be noted that the distinction between *de dictu* and *de re* necessity is different from the two sorts of necessity used in Anselm's texts (especially in *Cur Deus Homo*). Anselm distinguishes between antecedent and subsequent necessity. The former refers to a type of necessity that is coercive or provides constraint; it is a factual necessity rather than a logical necessity. Clearly this is not the sort of necessity involved in the ontological argument, not even regarding *de re* necessity. Subsequent necessity is logical rather than factual or coercive. It is the sort of necessity that is crucial in the ontological argument, especially when the necessity involved is inferential. Of course, in a metaphorical way one is forced to the conclusion of a tight rational argument, but the coercion here is intellectual rather than physical. Defenders of the ontological argument emphasize "subsequent necessity" when they claim that a careful consideration of the concept of God leads to the conclusion that God exists necessarily (Brecher 1985, 19–22). Knowledge of God's necessary existence is not thereby an exception to logical or metaphysical principles, but the result of them.

Despite the fact that the uses of necessity in Hartshorne, Malcolm, Plantinga, and other contemporary defenders of the ontological argument are somewhat different from the uses found in Anselm, it is crucial for defenders of the argument to resist the claim, dear to both Oppy and John Hick, that the question of whether there is an ontologically necessary being is a question of fact (Hick 1967, 353). Once again, the logic of perfection leads us to conclude that God's existence is either impossible or necessary in that it cannot be contingent, and this conclusion can be reached without appeal to any particular empirical observations. That is, the ontological argument is at odds with both Hick's empirical theism and Oppy's empirical religious skepticism. This does not mean, however, that the experiential "data" of religious experience that are emphasized by Hick are at odds with a defense of the ontological argument. Such experiences actually count in favor of the possibility of, hence the necessary existence of, God.

Joel Friedman is like Oppy in thinking that, because concreteness is contingent, the existence of a concrete God could never be necessary (Friedman 1980). The problem here is the assumption that the distinction between the abstract and the concrete maps without remainder on the distinction between the universal and the particular (or the individual). As Hartshorne sees things, the distinction between the abstract and the concrete coincides more closely with the distinction between existence and actuality. Actuality is the most concrete reality of a particular occasion in its coming-to-be, whereas existence is the abstract constant that marks the line of inheritance that applies to a common series of occasions.

Goodwin insightfully responds to Friedman (and indirectly to Oppy) regarding these distinctions:

> Friedman's remark that "concrete existence cannot be logically derived from definitions and meaning postulates alone" is ambiguous. If it means that particular concrete *actuality* cannot be deduced from meaning postulates, I agree. In all cases, divine and non-divine, concrete states are radically contingent.... If, however, the remark means that *existence* can never be logically derived from meaning postultates, I disagree. (Goodwin 1983, 223)

Friedman goes further than Oppy in claiming, in contrast to Goodwin, that there might have been nothing concrete in existence. That is, there might have been nothing at all. We have seen that the neoclassical view is that it is a necessary truth that there be contingency: "What is deduced from the ontological argument is the bare necessity of the divine existence, including the necessary truth that there be some or other concrete divine states, but not any particular state" (Goodwin 1983, 224; also Towne 1999, 243–248).

More Natural Language Considerations

Throughout I have been considering the existence of God via natural language. As modal notions have entered these considerations, they have done so via natural language, rather than through formal logic or through debates in contemporary semantics. It must be admitted, however, that I have followed Hartshorne and other neoclassical theists in construing God's necessary existence as obtaining in all possible worlds, which, once again, are possible or alternative states of the real world that we live in. No doubt Oppy would object as follows (Oppy 1995, 47–64, regarding definitional and conceptual versions of the ontological argument): even if God's existence must be *considered* necessary, it does not follow that God exists; or again, *if* God exists, this existence is necessary. Hartshorne responds to this sort of objection by saying:

> "If God exists, he exists noncontingently" I regard as self-contradictory; for the "if" can only mean that something which could be lacking is required for the existence, while "noncontingently" means that nothing required for the existence could possibly fail, or have failed to obtain. "If" refers to a condition, but we are speaking of unconditioned existence. Thus "if" and "necessary" do not properly combine in the manner proposed. (Hartshorne 1964, 347)

That is, "if" implies that God's nonexistence is possible, but "necessary" implies that God's nonexistence is impossible (Viney 1985, 49).

If one decides that modality is merely linguistic, one has, in effect, decided many of the most important metaphysical issues. It makes more sense to defend Peirce's view that time is objective modality, as we have seen Goodwin emphasize. Hartshorne sums up this view in the following terms:

The past is the mode of conditional or concrete necessity (being necessary, given the actual present), the future is the mixed mode of conditional necessity and possibility. So much for the distinction between necessity *de dictu* and necessity *de re*, logical and ontological necessity. The better our language, the more it reflects the real or temporal modalities into linguistic ones. (Hartshorne 1970, 253–254)

This theory of time as objective modality will probably receive the following criticism from Oppy and others when it is used to support the ontological argument: that one has made necessity of thought and necessity of existence identical. This criticism is problematic because there is, at the very least, a conceptual distinction between *de dictu* and *de re* necessity. Hartshorne carefully responded to this objection for almost eighty years: "because we must think something to be, it does not follow that it *actually* is" (Hartshorne 1923, 269–270 – emphasis added). The "leap" from thought to *existence* in the divine case is no great athletic feat; we should be skeptical, however, of anyone who claimed to leap from thought to *actuality*.

Critics of the ontological argument like Oppy, when they say that the argument is vacuous, or perhaps even tautological, fail to notice that the necessary existence of God demonstrated in the argument is not meant to show any particular feature of the world (as in "right now there is a deer in the backyard eating the flowers"), but only a purely general status of any possible world, viz., that it be deified. It cannot be emphasized too much in neoclassical theism that God's *existence* is not particular, although God's *actuality* is so indeed. The key question is whether the concept of God makes sense: "either worship is self-contradictory (rather than merely mistaken), or its object exists necessarily" (Hartshorne 1987, 79). This is quite different from saying that the mere use of a word establishes its necessity.

To say that a perfect being might exist conditionally is to contradict oneself. But to restrict the necessary existence of a perfect being to *de dictu* necessity is to impose such a condition. Unconditional necessity involves a *de re* component. To be precise, unconditional necessity can be applied indifferently to propositions or things:

A necessary proposition ... is strictly implied or included in the full meaning of any proposition, and analogously a necessary thing is one included in, constitutive of, any possible thing.... [This is] a necessity at once logical and ontological. (Hartshorne 1987, 79–80)

No doubt Oppy and other critics of the ontological argument are correct in claiming that necessity cannot relate concepts to actual things.

But please note, "exemplified property," "unexemplified property," "necessarily exemplified property," are all concepts, not particular existing things. Necessity can perfectly well relate the concept "perfection" to the concept "necessarily exemplified property." (Hartshorne 1962, 92)

God is not a "particular individual," *as least not as this phrase is normally used,* so as to refer to a being with a particular, fragmentary role to play in the cosmos. "Particular individual," in this sense, is not relevant to all others, nor are all others relevant to it, as God is.

The actuality of God is not deducible from the abstract necessity of God's existence. If the abstract necessity of God's existence as a logical possibility is not really possible, it must be due to the presence of something that gets in the way of the real existence: "But no positive or negative condition can be relevant to the existence of perfection, for conditioned existence is an imperfection" (Hartshorne 1962, 95). Once again, any hard distinction between logical and real possibility should be called into question. Suppose, for example, that a natural law prohibited a certain logically conceivable thing. This does not show, as many suspect it does, that there is an ultimate difference between logical and real possibility in that it is possible (even likely, over an immense stretch of time) that the natural law could change. There is nothing in the practice of scientists that dictates that natural laws be everlastingly valid. To put the issue in the strongest possible terms: necessity itself has a *theistic* meaning. Something is necessary only if God in all actual divine states experiences what it affirms; something is contingent if God may or may not experience what it affirms (Hartshorne 1962, 99).

Without the temporal theory of modality, it would make sense to say that it is still possible that "Dewey defeats Truman." But it makes even less sense to say this in 2004 than it did in 1948. Goodwin has argued (convincingly, I think) that the temporal interpretation of the modalities can be supported by the influential Kripke semantics, wherein, contra Oppy, "our actual world has a special indexed place in the series of possible worlds" (Hubbeling 1991, 364). To put the point in natural language terms, the temporal theory of modality provides the bridge between logic and metaphysics (Hartshorne 1991, 654). Without this theory, Oppy is right to press his general objection. Unfortunately, Oppy does not refute but ignores the theory of objective, temporal modality. This is unfortunate because if reality is perpetually enriched by new definiteness, then the step from the less to the more definite cannot be necessary (Hartshorne 1977, 163).

Although necessity has no role to play in divine actuality, it is central to divine existence. Relying on Hartshorne and Purtill (the latter of whom is nonetheless a critic of the ontological argument), we can develop the following position matrix that lays out the modal options regarding what we think about. If we think of something it is either:

1. existent (i.e., outside of the thinker's mind) and its nonexistence is inconceivable;
2. existent and its nonexistence is conceivable;
3. nonexistent and its existence is conceivable;
4. nonexistent and its existence is inconceivable.

Only the first option is tenable when thinking of deity. This is primarily because the second option encourages us to conceive of a superior to deity, which contradicts the Anselmian definition of deity as that than which no greater can be conceived. Further, the third option implies the conceivability of the second option; if the second option is contradictory when thinking of deity, the third goes down the tubes as well. It has already been admitted that the fourth option poses the most significant challenge to the ontological argument, hence the importance of developing a coherent concept of God when attempting to argue for the existence of God. In the present context, however, it is worth noting that the fourth option is counterintuitive precisely because we (theists as well as atheists and agnostics) *do* conceive of God (Hartshorne 1967c, 290). As before, exactly how is God's necessary existence like a square-circle?

Because only the first option is tenable, we should design language properly so as to reflect the ontological modalities, not the other way around. If there is no ontological impossibility, contingency, or necessity, then our modal terms are merely words about words:

The reason the affirmation of God's existence is subject only to necessary, rather than contingent, truth or falsity is that the ontological conditions for contingency are excluded by the definition of God, as they are for no other individual definition or concept. Indeed, God is the only individual being which is specifiable by a definition in purely general terms, devoid of empirical elements. (Hartshorne 1967c, 291)

That is, God is the one individual who, unlike localized individuals that are not specifiable by categories alone, is affected by and affects *every* other individual (Hartshorne 1967a, 40; 1948). It is because we really know what ontological possibility is that we can know what ontological necessity is. The necessary is "what is left when we have completely abstracted from the distinctive features of the various contingent alternatives" (Hartshorne 1967c, 292). Or again, "one must hold that there are no actual yet merely future cases, since the future is irreducibly modal, an affair of objective or extralinguistic possibilities, not actualities" (Hartshorne 1967c, 292–293).

Symmetry here is an illusion in that the past consists of those events that have actually occurred: "Modality is a mixture of creative freedom and conditioning by the past which *is* process" (Hartshorne 1967c, 293). We must therefore reject the idea that a contingent event has always existed; it has not always existed even in the mind of an ideal divine knower. This is because all contingency refers to at least partially indeterminate futurity, in some cases to past futurity:

If real possibility, as extralinguistic, is futurity, it should not be hard to say what necessity is. That which has always characterized the future in its aspect of will-be cannot be contingent. Thus, to find the unconditionally necessary we do not need to run through future events as particulars – how could that be done? – we need only ask whether the thing characterizes all past futures as common to their entire range of possibilities. (Hartshorne 1967c, 294)

When we speak of the necessary we mean the very abstract characteristics of becoming. That is, becoming can produce any number of actual things, but it cannot produce the utter absence of becoming:

What then does it mean to say that God, as unsurpassable by another, "cannot be conceived not to exist"? It does, of course, minimally imply that he is conceivable only as *always* existing; but to say this is not enough. We must say, God is conceivable, only as essential to becoming as such, hence to possibility as such. (Hartshorne 1967c, 294)

The assumption that necessity is a matter of propositions (is *de dictu* and not *de re*) is questionable if reality involves creative process with an aspect of futurity with its partial indeterminacy. On this latter view, the necessary is what all possible actual states have in common. For example, contingent knowers such as ourselves know some things and are quite ignorant of others; a necessary being who had ideal knowledge would know every actual state. We have seen, however (contra Oppy), the modesty of what is claimed here because from an abstract proposition only further abstract propositions can follow. In addition to "divinity exists necessarily," we can only conclude, as a result of the ontological argument, to other equally abstract propositions, as in the conclusion that God must know all that there is to know, but the outcomes to future contingencies are not here yet to be known. Oppy unfortunately, by way of contrast, buys into all of the classical theistic assumptions regarding the concept of God that neoclassical theism calls into question (Hartshorne 1965, 43–48).

In a way that he perhaps did not intend, Wittgenstein was correct in claiming that theology is grammar: God's existence is either a necessity or an impossibility and we speak inaccurately if we say that it is a contingent matter one way or the other. A necessary existent (rather than a *de dictu* necessity) can here be defined as an "existence which is affirmable in a necessarily true proposition" (Hartshorne 1965, 80). Although radical independence of *de dictu* and *de re* necessity might make sense with respect to conditional necessity, as described above, such independence does not make sense with respect to the sort of necessity with which the ontological argument is concerned: *unconditional* necessity. Regarding the concept of God, "necessary falsity is the only way in which it could fail to be true if it has any meaning at all" (Hartshorne 1965, 97).

I would like to conclude this chapter with one last Hartshornian effort to confront Oppy's general objection head-on. It will be objected that in the ontological argument *de dictu* and *de re* necessity have been confused; that *if* God exists, then God exists necessarily, but the assertion that God exists itself remains contingent. My response is that *de dictu* and *de re* necessity are closer than this objection indicates because of the unintelligibility of claiming of a perfect being that it exists necessarily *if* it exists. The "if it exists" premise indicates a conditional rather than an unconditional necessity, a conditional state that is inappropriate for the unsurpassable. That is, *de dictu* and *de re* necessity are coextensive only in the case of a being so perfect that anything less than unconditional necessity applied to its existence would contradict the very concept of perfection (Hartshorne 1965, 54, 79, 115).

There is an ambiguity here, however, that should be clarified. If the claim "if God exists, then God exists necessarily" is interpreted in a strictly ontological way, there does indeed appear to be a contradiction, as stated in the previous paragraph, in that the possibility of God failing to exist is at odds with God's existing necessarily. But if the claim involves both epistemological and ontological dimensions, the contradiction is avoided, as Viney insightfully argues. On this reasoning, the claim can be interpreted as saying that "if God exists but we are not sure if God exists, then God exists necessarily." The ontological meaning of "necessity" in the consequent does not contradict what goes on in the first part of the claim if the first part has an epistemological meaning. The defense of the ontological argument that I am offering in this book is one wherein it is freely admitted that the argument in itself does not tell us if the concept of God is coherent. This is an especially important concession in light of the fact that I see the traditional concept of God as incoherent.

5

Oppy, Perfect Islands, and Existence as a Predicate

In the previous chapter on Graham Oppy's important book, I tried to deal forthrightly with a standard objection to the ontological argument, reiterated by Oppy, that the ontological argument involves inappropriate talk about a necessary being. If only propositions can be necessary, it is alleged, then the ontological argument is (at least virtually) worthless. The following sort of response makes sense: *even if* necessity is applied only to propositions, the ontological argument shows that the proposition that "God's existence cannot be contingent" is true at all times and hence the argument is anything but worthless (cf. Purtill 1966, 406). Regardless of whether we take necessity to be *de dictu* or *de re* or both, however, it should be noted that there is no incompatibility between the conclusion of the ontological argument and the reported (contingent) empirical evidence of religious experience. As before, different strands of evidence can mutually reinforce each other (Johnson 1977).

The purpose of the present chapter, however, is to respond in greater detail to two familiar concerns of Oppy and other critics of the ontological argument: the perfect island objection made famous by Gaunilo and echoed in similar contemporary parody objections, on the one hand, and the existence is not a predicate objection made famous by Kant and found in similar contemporary objections, on the other. Oppy predictably supports parodies of the ontological argument, but he is surprisingly skeptical regarding existence is not a predicate objections.

Perfect Island Objections

Oppy takes Gaunilo to be offering, roughly and in abbreviated fashion, the following sort of argument:

A. An island than which no greater can be conceived can exist in the understanding.
B. If an island than which no greater can be conceived exists in the understanding, but does not exist in reality, then a greater island can be conceived that exists both in the understanding and in reality.
C. Hence an island than which no greater can be conceived does exist in reality (see Oppy 1995, 17–18).

Oppy takes this Gaunilo-like objection to be a parody of the ontological argument, an argument that he thinks deserves to be parodied. If one objects to this use of parody by saying that a perfect island is impossible because there is no way to accommodate everything we might desire of an island (more room, more trees, more Nubian maidens – to use Plantinga's example), Oppy would respond by claiming that what goes for islands goes for greatest conceivable beings, too, and for a greatest conceivable world: there could always be a greater. This seems to be Oppy's first objection to the efforts of defenders of the ontological argument to respond to Gaunilo-like criticisms.

Second, Oppy thinks that judgments about great-making properties are "irreducibly subjective." As he puts the point:

Conceiving is always conceiving *by* someone. What is conceivable is always what is conceivable *for* someone. It is a big step to suppose that there is a – greatly idealized – limit in which the conceivings – and judgments about conceivability – of all reasonable persons converge. (Oppy 1995, 167)

Such convergence, he predicts, will not likely occur if the notion of greatness involved relies on a Platonic or Neoplatonic metaphysics that contains greater or lesser degrees of existence. The obvious problem here, as Oppy sees things, is that one can reasonably doubt if there is a hierarchy of existence: "If the argument is taken to rely on Neoplatonic metaphysics, then it is completely lacking in probative force; there are very few nonbelievers who are committed to such a metaphysics" (Oppy 1995, 170).

Third, Oppy seems to agree with Tooley that the production of parodies of the ontological argument shows that modal ontological arguments, in particular (but why?), exhibit a type of argumentation that is structurally very much like arguments that lead to untenable conclusions (Tooley 1981; Chambers 2000). These parodies make the ontological argument itself dialectically ineffective (and presumably worthless), he thinks (Oppy 1995, 183–185).

Finally, Oppy explicitly relates his skepticism regarding rejoinders to the perfect island objection (and to other parodies of the ontological argument) to Hartshorne's philosophy. Perhaps we could interpret a perfect island to have Godlike properties even though it is not a part of the concept of God on either classical or neoclassical grounds to have an island-body. The purpose of the parody is nonetheless fulfilled, Oppy thinks, when it is considered that Hartshorne *does* defend a notion of divine embodiment of some sort (Oppy 1995, 318–319; Dombrowski 1988c).

What are we to make of these four objections? I will respond to them both here and in the following section.

The assumption made by defenders of the perfect island approach is that the ontological argument only establishes conceptual existence, not real existence. This assumption is mistaken. What the ontological argument establishes is that *if* God is conceivable, then the nonexistence of God is inconceivable; but conceiving of God is *not* the same as conceiving of a perfect island, a perfect devil, and so forth. An island, both by definition and in popular discourse, implies contingency, hence a perfect island implies a contradiction between something that is both necessary and not necessary. An ingenious objection like the perfect island one not only distorts, it altogether misses the main point of the ontological argument. Nonetheless, Gaunilo and Oppy are to be thanked for posing the relevant question regarding whether or not the form of the ontological argument can be applied to topics other than divine existence. It cannot (Hartshorne 1965, 19–21, 83).

What Anselm discovered was not that God is perfect in "His kind" in the way that a perfect island would be the best in "its kind." Rather, the defender of the ontological argument claims that God *is* "His kind" (if the male pronoun be momentarily permitted – "Her kind" would work as well). "Island" is a traditional kind, divine perfection is not; the concept of divine perfection is unique. The fact that no one (not even Gaunilo or Oppy) has ever believed in the existence of a perfect island is ultimately due to the fact that simply to be an island is a limitation. To get rid of the limitation altogether would be to get rid of the character of islandhood itself and any instantiation of it (Hartshorne 1965, 117–119).

A helpful metaphor goes as follows: Gaunilo and Oppy have not, like Samson, pulled down the pillars on the ontological argument from the inside; they have never really been inside the argument, only in a partially separable antechamber. Once again, however, Gaunilo and Oppy are nonetheless on to something important. They are legitimately suspicious of any effort to prove the concrete actuality of God from mere abstract reasoning. However, because they lack the distinction between divine existence and divine actuality, they illegitimately assume that their suspicion regarding divine actuality can be extended to the unprovability of divine existence (Hartshorne 1965, 152–153).

An island unsurpassable by any other island lacks a clear meaning, but an island unsurpassable by anything whatsoever is altogether meaningless. That is, to be *metaphysically* perfect is to be an exceptional case and "perfect island" cannot mean "metaphysically perfect island" in that an island's actuality (in contrast to God's actuality) could not be coincident with all actuality and an island's possibility (in contrast to God's possibility) could not be coincident with all possibility. Further, an island than which no greater could be conceived seems to have nothing in common with what anyone (not even Gaunilo or Oppy) means in everyday discourse by "island" or "dollars" or "thalers," to use a Kantian example (Hartshorne 1970, 249; 1962, 55–56, 62).

Parodies of the ontological argument in terms of a "perfect" devil or a "perfect" island fail because these cannot be coherently conceived due to the limitations involved in devilness and insularity, respectively. What could insular perfection mean? What could necessarily existing island mean if islands by their very definition and essence are imperfect and contingent affairs (Hartshorne 1944, 243; 1950, 45)?

Consider the following: a perfect devil would have to care for, with unrivaled attention, the lives of all sentient beings *and* yet hate all of them, with unrivaled bitterness. Such a being does not exist *and necessarily so.* Or again, a perfect island would require "waters" that never eroded its shores. But an island is competitive with other possibilities, as in its being eroded, even inundated, due to global warming. To be precise:

"Unsurpassable, necessary island" is nonsense. If "unsurpassable and necessary being" is also nonsense, then positivism is correct. But the nonsense could not be *for the same reason,* since "island" limits perfection while "being" does not. (Hartshorne 1983, 101; also 1941, 303–304)

It is one thing to believe in the cosmos as the embodiment of God's omniscient care over all being, it is quite another to have the cosmos identified with a particular thing like an island.

It should now be clear how one can respond to Oppy's objections. The first objection pushes the perfect island idea together with that than which no greater can be conceived; but the dramatic differences between these two make it extremely difficult to push them together in this fashion. Second, the fact that neither Gaunilo nor Oppy nor the defender of the ontological argument believes in a perfect island is indicative of the fact that concepts of perfection are not merely subjective and are not as relativistic as Oppy suggests. Third, because the concept of a perfect island is not at all like the concept of that than which no greater can be conceived, the fact that the former leads to an untenable conclusion need not have any negative effect on the latter, as Oppy suggests. And fourth, divine embodiment, if there is such, would be cosmic in scope and would not be exhausted by, nor identified with, a particular body like an island.

One reason to take parodies of the ontological argument seriously is that it is but a short step from Oppy-like parody to Michael Martin's and Stephen Davis' apparent belief that the ontological argument is, as Schopenhauer put it, a charming joke. They seem to think that it is a joke because they, along with J. L. Mackie, believe that it is just obvious that one cannot "prove the existence of any concrete reality by an entirely a priori procedure" (Davis 2003, 103–104; also Martin 1990; Mackie 1982). In a way, Davis is quite right! Notice the following ambiguity: if he is talking about divine (concrete) actuality, he is correct; but if he is talking about (abstract) divine existence, he is quite mistaken. Like many philosophers of religion, Davis claims to have read Hartshorne carefully, but he ignores altogether one of Hartshorne's key contributions to scholarship on the ontological argument: the distinction between existence and actuality.

Michael Gettings is astute to see the affinity between Oppy's approach to the ontological argument and Gaunilo's approach (Gettings 1999; cf. Haight and Haight 1970; Kane 1984; Richman 1958; Grant 1957). The strategy is to question whether "God-likeness" applies only to God or to many theologically misleading entities such as demigods, islands, devils, less than perfect beings, and so on. The ontological argument is meant to demonstrate that "God-likeness" implies that a being who is Godlike has as essential properties not only good properties, but all and only the best properties. Gettings is correct that even a "perfect" island is still an island with something less than the best properties (as in contingent rather than necessary existence).

The same point is made by Philip Devine, who relies on St. Bonaventure (*De Mysterio Trinitatis* I, 1). To say that a being than which no greater can be conceived exists necessarily is to say nothing such that the subject and the predicate conflict. But to speak of an island than which no greater can be conceived *is* to produce a contradiction between the subject and the predicate if "island" refers to a contingent or defective thing, whereas the predicate designates perfection. Strange as it seems, and against his intent, Oppy reverts to an invidious Platonism here. An *island* is necessarily subject to contingencies and defects; only the Platonic form of *islandhood* could be proposed (erroneously) as perfect; but islandhood is not an island (see Devine 1975a, 256; Burgess-Jackson 1994). Oppy would here seem to be committing what Whitehead calls the fallacy of misplaced concreteness. Even greater difficulties face the parody of the ontological argument based on the perfect devil, where the contradiction can be detected rather easily even by those who have not thought very much about the matter.

Oppy and the Existence Is Not a Predicate Objection

Oppy is helpful in distinguishing between at least two different objections to the ontological argument in Kant's first critique: (a) the objection that no existence claims are analytic; and (b) the objection that existence is not a predicate. This second objection sometimes surfaces in the related objection that negative existentials are never self-contradictory (A595/B623). I would like to deal briefly with the first of these objections, then at length with the second.

It was noted earlier that Kant appears not to have ever read Anselm's versions of the ontological argument. Rather, he was familiar only with a Carte*sian* version of the argument. But it is questionable whether he ever read Descartes' version, either. That is, his knowledge of the ontological argument seems to have been derived from rationalists like Christian Wolff (Oppy 1995, 29–39; Everitt 1995). One can legitimately wonder whether Kant was attacking a straw man. One can wonder as well about Feuerbach's criticisms of the argument, which seem to rely exclusively on the weaker, nonmodal version of the argument. Further, his criticisms of the argument seem to rely, as do Kant's, on the unquestioned assumption that classical theism just *is* theism (Feuerbach 1957, 36, 198–200).

Oppy thinks that the weaker of the two Kantian objections is the one that is primarily derived from Hume, as discussed in Chapter 1. This is the objection that no existence claims are analytic (A7/B11). An analytic claim is one where the predicate "belongs to" the subject. Kant thinks not only that no existence claims can be analytic, but also that no synthetic claims can be established via a purely logical argument. So the onto-logical argument will not work in that this argument violates both of these principles. Oppy is understandably not impressed with this objection primarily because of the possible counterargument provided in the ontological argument itself! That is, Oppy is commendably wary of attempts to refute the ontological argument by simply legislating it out of contention as a sound argument.

The stronger of the two Kantian objections, according to Oppy, is found in the slogan that "existence is not a predicate." To say that existence is not a real predicate (A598/B626–A600/B628) is to say that it is not a concept of something that could be added to (a concept of) a thing. It is merely the positing of the thing. In effect, it is only the copula of a judgment. An example from Kant himself is that the proposition "God is omnipotent" has two concepts: God and omnipotence. The word "is" adds no new predicate, but serves only to posit the predicate in relation to the subject.

It is well known that Kant was a defender of the Aristotelian logic that was supplanted by Frege and Russell. But Kant's point can easily be put in their terms: the existential quantifier must be attached to a predicate expression or to a general description. Only when this is done will the sentence say something. That is, without this combination of features, the sentence will not really say anything (Oppy 1995, 33; Nussbaum 1994).

Despite the fact that this is the stronger of the two Kantian objections to the ontological argument, Oppy is not convinced that Kant has adequately defended this objection (Oppy 1995, 38). The idea here is that no list of all the properties to be attributed to even a complete concept of a thing will include the existence of that thing. This is because, on the Kantian view, the existence of a thing is a matter of its being *related to* the complete concept of that thing. Existence, on this interpretation of Kant, is not one of the intrinsic (i.e., nonrelational) properties of a thing. On this view, existence is necessarily relational.

Oppy floats the hypothesis that existence could in fact be one of the real properties of things. This is not to say that he believes this hypothesis, but rather that he is not convinced by Kant's arguments in favor of the existence is not a predicate slogan (Oppy 1995, 35–38). What should be noted in all of this is that Oppy, like Kant, in a certain sense carries on his discussion in nonmodal terms: he focuses on whether existence, rather than necessary existence, is a predicate. As Oppy sees things, necessary existence and contingent existence are *nothing other than* types of existence. Likewise, Oppy treats divine existence and divine actuality as roughly synonymous (Oppy 1995, 211–212, 229). These foci are problematic. Nonetheless, Oppy surprisingly agrees with Hartshorne that an ideal cannot have a clear and consistent meaning and yet be utterly incapable of existence. Although this is a step toward the ontological argument on Oppy's part, it is obviously not to be construed as a commitment to it (Oppy 1995, 274).

Unlike most opponents of the ontological argument, Oppy suggests (albeit tentatively) that there are senses in which existence *is* a predicate. Words like "exists" and "is" can clearly function as *grammatical* predicates in sentences that have a subject-predicate form. The key question seems to be, can existence function as a *logical* predicate as well (cf. Moore 1965)? Oppy seems to agree with Frege and Russell that existence is a logical predicate in the sense of it being a *second-order predicate*. That is, the properties of *objects* are first-order predicates (e.g., mammalian properties can be predicated of horses), whereas the properties of *concepts*, such as existence, are second-order predicates. To say that horses exist is not really to say anything about particular horses such as Seattle Slew. Rather, it is to say that the concept of "horse" is instantiated (Oppy 1995, 130–131, 145).

To admit that existence can be a grammatical predicate as well as a second-order logical predicate still does not assure us that we are in a position to defend the ontological argument, according to Oppy. This is because defenders of the ontological argument would probably deny that the proposition that horses exist says nothing whatsoever about horses. They ask, why should we agree with Frege that "exists" should always be analyzed as a second-order predicate? Further, even if there is a second-order existence predicate, does this automatically rule out the option that there is a first-order existence predicate? (Forgie 1972; Oppy 1995, 309–315).

Quine's skepticism is related to Frege's. That is, Quine sees a very close connection between existence and quantification, as in his famous saying that "To be is to be a value of a bound variable" (Quine 1963). One can ask: "Why must this be the case?"

The questions asked in the previous two paragraphs lead Oppy to claim that if the ontological argument is threatened, it is not due to the existence is not a predicate slogan. As before, if Oppy is to be faulted here it is, in part, because he does not relate his criticisms of this slogan to the crucial modal distinction between necessary and contingent existence. It is the former that outranks the latter when dealing with a perfect being and that is crucial for the argument to work (Oppy 1995, 152).

Oppy's contribution here lies in his realization that what the existence is not a predicate objectors to the ontological argument want is a sense in which "exists" is separated from all other predicates because it does not express a property. One way to have this wish granted is to defend what amounts to nominalism, wherein one stipulates that existence is not a predicate. But becoming a nominalist is a very high price to pay in order to refute the ontological argument. Another way to accomplish the same goal is to stipulate that what exists is what scientists tell us (contingently) exists. Oppy is clearly bothered by nominalism, yet he is curiously tolerant of the abdication of responsibility exhibited by those who give scientists a carte blanche regarding existence claims (Oppy 1995, 156–159, 231–235, 299–301, 306–310).

A convenient summary of Oppy's view on the existence is not a predicate thesis can be found in the following quotation, a quotation that serves the admirable function of eliminating confusion regarding his nuanced overall stance:

> it should be stressed that it is not really important to my purposes that it turn out that existence *is* a predicate; it will suffice if I have managed to show that it is very difficult to decide whether or not existence is a predicate. . . . What I really want to defend is the idea that it is sensible to try to provide compelling reasons for refusing to pay any more attention to ontological arguments without so much as taking up the question whether existence is a predicate. (Oppy 1995, 160–161)

Once again, despite Oppy's insightful comments regarding why it is not easy to defend the claim that existence is not a predicate, in the final analysis he is fixated on the worthlessness of the ontological argument. My own view, by way of contrast, is that the worth of the ontological argument becomes apparent, in part, when it is realized that the existence is not a predicate mantra is not as obviously true as it once seemed. That is, Oppy is actually to be thanked for helping to make matters more complex than they once seemed (cf. Cornman 1987; Mackie 1976; Williams 1981). He is also correct to mention, although he does not explore this point in any detail, that once various modes of existence are introduced the existence is not a predicate slogan looks quite different (Oppy 1995, 315; cf. Everitt 2004, 51–57).

Neoclassical Theism and the Existence Is Not a Predicate Objection

A neoclassical theistic response to the existence is not a predicate objection can build on Oppy's skepticism regarding this objection, but it also goes beyond Oppy's approach in at least two ways. First, greater attention needs to be paid to the distinction between necessary and contingent existence and how this distinction facilitates the effort to counteract the objection under consideration. And second, the use of a position matrices approach to the ontological argument, entirely ignored by Oppy, should be considered in the effort to thoroughly understand the relationship between necessary existence and predication in the ontological argument. It will be the purpose of this section of the chapter to explore these two areas.

Consider the following position matrix, which lays out the logically possible positions that are available when considering the conceivability of deity in relation to the variables "existent" or "nonexistent":

A. Deity cannot be consistently conceived.
B. Deity can be consistently conceived, equally whether as existent or as non-existent.
C. Deity can be consistently conceived, but only as nonexistent, as a . . . regulative ideal or limiting concept.
D. Deity can be consistently conceived, but only as existent (Hartshorne 1970, 281).

It must be admitted that (A) is not obviously wrong and that, if there were no other arguments for the existence of God and no pervasive history of people claiming to have had religious experiences, then the denial of the conceivability of God would make more sense. However, there *are* other arguments for the existence of God and there *is* a long history, spread across the globe, of claims of having had religious experiences, hence it is plausible to think that God's existence is at least conceivabile.

The problematic nature of (B) lies in the assumption that the greatest conceivable being (God) could be a merely possible being, a being whose existence is causally conditioned. The reason why such a conception is inconsistent with that than which no greater can be conceived is that if God's existence *depends on* causal conditions, then the absence of such contingent conditions would *prevent* the greatest conceivable being from existing, in which case it would not be the greatest conceivable being: a contradiction.

The defects in (B) infect (C) as well. Another defect is that (C) involves a concept of God that is overly apophatic. If one hyperbolizes the sense in which God is not understood by us (apophatic or negative theology), one ends up with either atheism or agnosticism. But what if divine omniscience, say, is truly separated from us as inadequate knowers, in one sense, and quite intelligible to us, in another sense? That is, although we can understand the *concept* of divine omniscience, we cannot know in *actual* specificity what it would be like in concrete detail to know all other actualities. In effect, there is no reason why we have to defend a concept of God that relies *exclusively* on apophatic or negative theology; in addition, we can rely on a kataphatic or positive notion of divine perfection.

Given the inadequacies of (A), (B), and (C), and given the assumption that the four alternatives mentioned above are logically exhaustive (given the two variables of conceivability/inconceivability and existent/nonexistent), (D) seems to be the most defensible option.

The words "most defensible" need explication. The intent here is to mediate between two extremes: Oppy's stance that arguments for the existence of God, even the search for arguments for the existence of God, are vain or worthless, on the one hand, and the stance of some religious dogmatists that arguments for the existence of God can be entirely satisfactory and complete, on the other. The admission that (A) is not obviously wrong distances my view from the latter extreme stance. Kant, the first explicit defender of the existence is not a predicate objection, and Oppy lean decidedly in the direction of the former extreme stance.

A moderate stance allows one to readily admit that *any* argument can be rejected as long as one is willing to pay the price of such rejection, say by refusing to accept one of the premises or by defending one of the alternatives in a position matrix that is initially rejected. One should ask: in the position matrix, which alternative among (A), (B), or (C) should be resuscitated? Perhaps (A) should be resuscitated *if* the classical concept of God is assumed, with all of its contradictions (Hartshorne 1970, 275–278, 291; cf. Van Inwagen 1998; Hardy 1996).

The ontological argument, even in a position matrix formulation, is not refuted by the principle that *if* a perfect being exists, it exists necessarily. This is because it is contradictory to speak of something that non-necessarily exists as necessary. That is, the phrase "if a perfect being is *conceivable*" is quite different from the phrase "if a perfect being *exists*." The latter is problematic in ways that the former is not. It might be claimed that a defender of the ontological argument is still in deep trouble because it is being assumed that existence is a predicate. One can respond to this objection by saying that the difference between *contingent* existence and *necessary* existence allows one to predicate in a grammatically correct and (first-order) logical way (Hartshorne 1944, 233–234).

Consider the fact that this view is not as far from the Kantian one as may first appear to be the case. Kant may be correct that to say that "the ball is" is not really to predicate anything of the ball, in contrast to saying that "the ball is blue," where something (blueness) is clearly predicated of the ball. However, Kant, ignorant as he was of Anselm's two quite different versions of the ontological argument, did not consider an analogous contrast between "God is" (which gives rise to the existence is not a predicate theme) and "God is necessarily." It may be the case that to say that something exists or that it exists contingently is to offer a predicate only in an innocuous (i.e., grammatical) sense. But to say that something exists necessarily is anything but innocuous; this *is* to predicate something significant about the subject matter in question (Hartshorne 1967b, 324–325; cf. Hick 1967, 212–215).

Or more precisely regarding Kant, in addition to the well-known passages on the ontological argument in the first critique, in Kant's "Lectures on the Philosophical Doctrine of Religion" he does *mention* necessary existence, but he does so in order to illustrate the concept of *ens realissimum* (i.e., most real being) and not to reexamine the existence is not a predicate theme and not to contrast it with contingent existence or impossibility. On Kant's view, the concept of *ens realissimum* involves the idea that God contains all realities in itself without functioning as a World Soul.

Further, we have seen that the ontological argument shows that a merely contingent exemplification of divinity would be contradictory. That is, "not thinking" divinity (in the sense of thinking of something other than divinity, as in the upcoming football game) is quite different from "thinking not" if divine nonexistence is strictly unknowable and if divine contingent existence is contradictory. One misunderstands the best versions of the ontological argument if one assumes that it concludes to a conception of God as existent. An important step is made toward a proper understanding of the argument if it is realized that God is being conceived as existentially noncontingent: either as impossible or as necessary. As Hartshorne puts the point in a quotation that brings together his opposition to both perfect island objections and existence is not a predicate objections:

if to be conceivable as not existing is a defect, then so in a sense is simply not existing, inasmuch as what is not existent is also conceivable as not existent. But non-existence is thereby shown to be a defect solely in comparison with what is inconceivable as non-existent. Since dollars or islands (the examples which have fascinated so many) are always conceivable as non-existent, there is no implication that existing dollars are greater than non-existent ones. The defect of contingency goes with being a dollar. (Hartshorne 1962, 58–59)

There is an interesting connection being made here that has hitherto gone unnoticed: the main problem with the perfect island objection is related to the main problem with the existence is not a predicate objection. The latter is plausible only in the absence of the distinction between contingent and necessary existence; the former is plausible only in the absence of the realization that islands, like dollars, are by definition contingent things. Modal indifference or modal confusion underlie both objections.

A neoclassical theist need not tolerate these absences. Ultimately the neoclassical view is quite different from Kant's view, whose modal theory is actually inferior to Aristotle's. The well-known distinction in Aristotle between the temporal as contingent and the eternal as necessary is close to the process view that I think should be defended: it is the past that is actual, it is the future that is possible, it is the present that is becoming actualized; the necessary is that which is ubiquitous throughout time. This is also the Peircian view of time as objective modality (Hartshorne 1983, 176).

By way of contrast, Kant's view seems to be: that it is the phenomenally necessary that is *required by* causal laws; and that it is the phenomenally possible that is *compatible with* causal laws. But what is noumenally necessary or possible we cannot strictly speaking know. This is the real reason, it seems, why Kant was opposed to the ontological argument, which, once again, he associated not with Anselm's versions, nor even with Descartes' or Leibniz's versions, but with the versions of Baumgarten or Wolff (Hartshorne 1983, 177).

The natural mechanism that Kant assumed to be the case in the first critique dictated that future events were necessary, once again in contrast to the biologically based modal asymmetry in Aristotle. On the latter view, the past is settled, but sentient animals, at least, still have to act in the present so as to influence what will happen in the future. On the deterministic view of Kant's first critique, however, there is a certain symmetry in that causal implications obtain equally whether going backward or forward in time. And even by the time of the third critique, Kant still associated conceptual knowledge with a mechanistic and deterministic world.

Not only is it misleading to say that existence is not a predicate, something close to the opposite is the case: the *mode* of a thing's existence (its impossibility or its contingency/necessity of existence) seems to be included in *every* predicate. In the divine case, mere possibility or contingency of existence drops out as an option, contra Kant and Oppy. In effect, Kant's mistake, only partially remedied by Oppy, was in arguing that there can be no contradiction in supposing the absence of any thing along with its predicates; contradiction can occur only when supposing the presence of some thing with contradictory predicates (Hartshorne 1941, 306–307, 313–319, 336).

The grammatical affinity among "God exists" and "A tiger exists" and "Satan exists" can easily mislead us if the modal distinctions involved in the logic of perfection are not considered. Of course we should talk grammatically about deity. But to admit this much is not to deny that, whereas ordinary (contingent) existence is not a predicate, contingency as such and necessary existence are predicates in the sense that they are meaningful and informative attributions to the subject in question. To say that God's existence is better than God's nonexistence is not exactly to capture the meaning of the ontological argument. Rather, we should say that the necessarily existent is better than the nonexistent in that contingency of existence is a defect *in a perfect being,* as is impossibility of existence (Hartshorne 1965, 73–76, 99).

My belief is that the ontological argument refutes atheism and that some other argument or experience can show the plausibility of the concept of God, thereby calling into question agnosticism. This belief would be thwarted if Kant is correct that contrasts like that between necessity and contingency transcend our experience and hence our conceptual knowledge. However, it seems that Kant, like Hume, places his skeptical conclusion in his initial assumptions. He does not really demonstrate, but assumes, that God must either be perceived in a sensory way or be inaccessible to conceptual knowledge. If Kant's point is that the *actual* cannot follow from any concept or definition, then surely he is correct. But the necessity of God found in the ontological argument concerns *existence,* specifically the abstract proposition that God must always exist in some actual state or other (Hartshorne 1965, 85, 208–227).

In a direct response to Kant's first critique, Hartshorne puts the matter in the following terms:

We do not "add" existence to the "bare possibility of God," we deny that this latter phrase has a consistent meaning. Nor do we "add to our concept" of God in affirming His existence; for the only proper concept of God is *as* existent. He can have no other status. (Hartshorne 1965, 228)

Further, Kant's assumption that God is the *ens realissimum* can also be called into question. The ontological argument:

... need not, and in neoclassical use does not, take God to be the actual union of all possible realities, the *ens realissimum*, but only the actual union of all actual realities, and the potential union of all possible ones *so far as mutually compossible*. (Hartshorne 1965, 229)

The main idea here is that it is divine concreteness or actuality that is hard for us to grasp, in contrast to the abstractness of God's necessary existence. Kant, like Oppy and unlike Hume, assumes that theism has to mean classical theism, where the distinction between existence and actuality is not made. Without this distinction, the permanence of divine existence is assumed to apply to God's concrete actuality as well.

In the neoclassical view, one gets a quite different picture:

Only if there is a real contrast between the determinate past and the determinable future can we have a basis for the concept of real possibility, of which real necessity is the most general or abstract aspect. Here is the crux of the modal problem. (Hartshorne 1965, 232)

I admit that Kant was correct in claiming that the key to coming to grips with our concepts is in the temporal structure of our experience, but his determinism in the first critique regarding our conceptual knowledge of nature makes this temporal structure unintelligible. And I also admit that Kant was correct in tracing all of the arguments for the existence of God back to the ontological one. Understanding the necessary existence of God does not seem to involve the sort of sensory experiences listed in a lab report. But it *does* involve being clear about: the asymmetrical nature of time; the modal distinctions among impossibility, possibility (or contingency), and necessity; and the distinctions among divine essence, existence, and actuality. It is this last set of distinctions that I will now examine in detail.

Essence, Existence, Actuality

We have seen that existence refers to the fact *that* God exists, whereas actuality refers to *how* God exists, to whatever contingent state or other in which God exists. Or again, divine actuality deals with the fact that God exists *somehow*, in some condition or other that is compatible with perfection. We can make a similar distinction with respect to human beings, but only in the divine case is the existence in question characterized by unconditional necessity rather than by contingency (Hartshorne 1970, 294–295).

For centuries philosophers were accustomed to speak in terms of the distinction between essence (*what* a thing is) and existence. Neoclassical theists can expand on this base so as to include actuality as well. This expansion is due to the desire to account for the distinction between the necessary embodiment of perfection in *some* concrete state or other (existence) and the particular state itself (actuality). That is, there is a difference between an individual's abstract identity and its concrete actual states. These divine states themselves involve contingency even if the fact that there are such states is necessary: "Perfection is not a class of similar individuals, but only a class of singular and genetically related states of one individual" (Hartshorne 1962, 65–67; 1990, 337).

Critics of the ontological argument are correct that it is impossible to deduce the divine actuality or the fullness of divine reality from an abstract formula or from a definition of divinity. From mere abstractions only abstract conclusions can follow. On this view, the abstractness of divine existence is, in a way, impoverished in that God's reality involves more than divine existence. It also includes a wealth of contingent qualities. As we have seen Hartshorne put the point:

... each moment my personal experience is concretized anew, but just how, in just what experiences, is always an additional fact, not deducible from the bare truth that I continue existing. Moreover, my individuality might not have been, and I might soon not be, concretized in any way at all. The divine individuality, by contrast, has this unique superiority: it must always be and have been concretized somehow. Only the *how*, not the *that* is here contingent. (see Hartshorne's "Introduction" in Anselm 1982, 17)

Or again, if "Es" stands for essence, if "Ex" stands for existence, if "Ac" stands for actuality, if " = " stands for "is equivalent to," and if "<" stands for "is less than," then the following is being claimed by the neoclassical theist *in the divine case*:

$$Es = Ex < Ac$$

In the nondivine case, of course, essence is not equivalent to existence (see Hartshorne's "Introduction" in Anselm 1982, 17–18).

The necessary, which does not become, is an abstraction from concrete reality. The ontological argument need not commit the blunder that legitimately concerns Oppy and others of deriving something concrete from an abstract definition. God's concrete actuality is contingent and is therefore undemonstrable. To escape several of Oppy's criticisms we need to persistently distinguish the *that* from the *how* of divine reality (Hartshorne 1963b, 290).

We have seen both that modality of existence is always a predicate and that contingency of existence contradicts categorical supremacy. Necessity of *existence* means the absence of a possible alternative, whereas contingency of *actuality* means the presence of possible alternatives. The necessary existence of God is not all of God. As the above equation indicates, the divine essence entails divine existence *plus* something. God's essence/existence provides something of an outline for divine reality (and outlines can be very instructive), but an outline is far less than the filled-in character of divine reality. This "filling-in" occurs at each divine present, as some possibilities rather than others in the near future are in the process of becoming actualized as a result of divine decisions – once again, literally the cutting off of certain possibilities (Hartshorne 1950, 40–45).

It will profit us to return for a moment to the existence is not a predicate objection so as to further clarify the differences between existence and actuality. It will be remembered that the weaker version of the ontological argument found in Anselm involved the idea that existence *extra mentem* is good, hence the best conceivable being had to have it. I have explored above the question regarding what it means to say that this sort of existence is not a predicate. Two possible positions should be avoided: existence is never a predicate and existence is always a predicate. These two responses, it should be noted, are contraries rather than contradictories. That is, if they are both false (as I think they are) we can still search for other alternatives (Hartshorne 1983, 93–95).

We have seen that some defensible alternatives include the following: existence is a grammatical predicate, existence is (at the very least) a second-order logical predicate, and (most importantly) modality of existence is always a predicate. Regarding the *impossibility* modality we can see that existence is not consistently conceivable, as in "round square." Regarding the *contingency* modality we can see that existence and nonexistence are equally conceivable. And regarding the *necessity* modality we can see that only existence is conceivable. A necessary existent would be one whose nonexistence is inconceivable, as in the stronger version of the ontological argument found in Anselm. It is precisely the inconceivability of the nonexistence of a perfect being that undercuts the contingency implied in Oppy's objection that God's existence is necessary *if* God exists. As Hartshorne puts the point: "The conceivability of theism is the real issue. The rest is misunderstanding" (Hartshorne 1983, 96–97). God's *existence* cannot have conditions, even if God's *actuality* can (indeed, must) have conditions. The idea of deity cannot fail to be realized in existence somehow, but the precise character of this existence has to wait upon decisions, both divine and nondivine.

Unfortunately, the confusion of existence with actuality is exhibited not only in religious skeptics like Oppy. There is a long line of classical theists who make the same mistake. Anselm himself deduced from the unchanging necessity of God's existence the unchanging actuality of God's reality in general. In a processual world, where new realities come into existence at each moment, the *how* of divine reality (i.e., divine actuality) cannot be deduced even if bare existence can be (Hartshorne 1983, 98–99, 102).

We will see in Chapter 6 that contemporary classical theists do as much to foster misunderstanding of the best versions of the ontological argument as do skeptics like Oppy. These versions require, at the very least, the triad essence/existence/actuality rather than the dichotomy essence/existence. Many theists dogmatically assert that God just has to be necessary in every respect. In the next chapter I will examine why. Why not claim that existence is merely a relation of exemplification that actuality has to essence? That is, only an aggressive sort of Leibnizian would insist on the rational derivability of *everything* (Hartshorne 1965, x–xi, 68, 131, 186).

There is a unique relation between the essence and the necessary existence of God; it is on this relation that the ontological argument logically turns. This uniqueness is due to the attenuated list of modal options in the divine case: contingent existence drops out as a viable alternative. Only impossibility and necessity of existence remain as viable alternatives. Therefore, if God does not exist there is not even a possibility that God exists (cf. Wild 1950). Or again, if God's existence is "merely" possible, then God exists necessarily: "Perfection cannot have the dependent relation to other things implied by the status of mere possibility" (Hartshorne 1941, 309).

Perhaps it will be objected by Oppy and others that no "mere" idea of God can reach existence, that only experience can do that. A partial response to this objection would include the observation that an idea *is* an experience of a certain kind, with the idea of perfection being a very particular sort of experience that has to be taken seriously. That is, the idea of perfection elicits in us the realization that in the case of God there is no distinction between the not impossible and the existent (Hartshorne 1941, 299–300, 310–311).

Another objection to the argument is that if God is, on neoclassical grounds, everlasting rather than eternal, then God's existence is contingent because all temporal phenomena are contingent. But this objection, once again, confuses existence and actuality. One can easily agree that God's actuality at any moment or other is contingent without subscribing to the idea that the very existence of such a divine being is contingent (Herrera 1979, 115; cf. Nelson 1963). Granted, it may *seem* that a concrete, temporal actuality is being deduced from an abstract definition in the ontological argument, but this is not the case in neoclassical versions of the argument. To *declare* that bare existence is never deducible is, in effect, to say that God is impossible. But why? The step from essence to existence is quite different from the step from (necessary) existence to actuality. It must be admitted, however, that in the case of beings whose existence *is* contingent, the step from essence to existence is by no means guaranteed. It is perhaps this legitimate point that fuels much illegitimate criticism of the ontological argument (Hartshorne 1967b, 329–333).

6

Rival Concepts of God and the Ontological Argument

Thomas Morris, Katherin Rogers, and Alvin Plantinga

In this final chapter of the book I would like to examine three analytic philosophers who are favorably disposed toward the ontological
argument: Thomas Morris, Katherin Rogers, and Alvin Plantinga. But
these thinkers defend Anselmian reasoning both in terms of Anselm's
argument for the existence of God and in terms of Anselm's problematic
concept of God. I will indicate why the neoclassical concept of God not
only is superior to Anselm's classical concept, but also facilitates a defense
of the ontological argument. That is, I will argue that the defenses of the
ontological argument by Morris, Rogers, and Plantinga are not likely to
withstand certain criticisms from the likes of Rorty, Taylor, and Oppy.

Morris's Anselmian Explorations and Rogers'
Perfect Being Theology

Morris commends the efforts of neoclassical theists to apply philosophical reasoning to religious belief, efforts that counteract the enormous
influence of Kantian fideism over the last two centuries. He locates two
points at which neoclassical theists make genuine progress. First, they are
right, he thinks, to call into question the classical theistic metaphysics that
is based on static categories (e.g., being rather than becoming, substance
rather than event, etc.) that are at odds with the dynamic tenor of the biblical God. And second, these static categories make it difficult to render
theistic belief consistent with the dynamism of concepts in contemporary
biology, physics, and other sciences (Morris 1987, 124–126).

Morris emphasizes the need to have a concept of God that is compatible with the dynamism of the world as described by science (especially

by evolutionary theory in biology). This need is emphasized as well by John Haught. In this regard philosophical theists have had a tendency to concentrate too much on the intelligent design of nature in an original creation (*creatio originalis*) at the expense of a continuous creation (*creatio continua*) throughout evolutionary history. However, God is not being redefined by Haught so as to fit a Darwinian view of the world. Rather, Haught is interested in the metaphysical and theological concept that he thinks is crucial in order to understand Christianity, in particular, and philosophical theism, in general, themselves: the kenotic emptying that lies behind the boundless, omnibenevolent divine love.

It must be admitted, however, that part of Haught's Hartshornian task, at least partially compatible with Morris's own task, is to develop a concept of God that fits the obvious contingency of much that happens in nature. Participants in evolutionary history meander, strive, and sometimes fail. (From the point of view of Plantinga's Calvinist determinism, however, this contingency is not obvious in that according to his theory, every act of predation in nature, say, was incredibly foreknown and caused – or at least permitted – by God.) The block universe of the deterministic Newtonian world (vestiges of which can be found in Morris, to a lesser extent in Rogers, but especially in Plantinga) is now a thing of the past among scientists. Contingency is not merely a mask for a hidden necessity, on Haught's instructive view. Necessity consists in the abstract constraints shared by all concrete and contingent existents (Haught 2000, 36–43, 100–102).

Ultimately, however, despite neoclassical theism's commendable dynamism, Morris sees neoclassical theism as a wolf in sheep's clothing. This is for two reasons. The first is that neoclassical theists defend the (heterodox) view that God needs the world, a view that is at odds with the (orthodox) belief that God freely created the world *ex nihilo*. The second defect that Morris sees in neoclassical theism (or at least in Hartshorne's version of it) concerns the concept of God's preservation of the world in divine memory, which acts as a substitute for subjective immortality. We will see that the first of these criticisms involves a rejection of the distinction between existence and actuality, whereas the second ironically involves a challenge to divine sovereignty. The irony is that it is usually classical theists like Morris, with their belief in divine omnipotence, who claim that neoclassical theists do not sufficiently emphasize divine sovereignty (Morris 1987, 127–129).

It can be agreed that God is that than which no greater can be conceived; the disagreement concerns what exactly this perfection involves. To be more specific, a neoclassical theist can agree with Morris that "it

is greater not to be dependent on anything else . . . than to be so dependent" when God's very existence is in question. But there is disagreement
regarding whether this independence is a greatness when God's loving
actuality is in question (Morris 1987, 130).

We should not confuse Morris's view with a more extreme version
of classical theism wherein God's *absolute* immutability is defended. He
resides in a place halfway between this extreme version of classical theism
and neoclassical theism. He disagrees with the extreme version of classical
theism, in part, because it conflicts with the biblical portrayal of a God
who responds both to creaturely suffering and to the spiritual discipline
of human beings. The God of the Bible and the neoclassical God offer
*re*sponses to creaturely suffering rather than the "*inde*sponses" (to use
Richard Creel's term) of an eternal, classical theistic God completely
outside of time. But Morris makes two distinctions that still keep him
some distance from neoclassical theism.

The first distinction is the Thomistic one between real and relational
change. An example of relational change would be to have someone
who was two miles to the east of a certain person move to a point three
miles to the east of this person without this person realizing it. Classical
theists typically claim that all changes in God are merely relational (or
extrinsic) and not real (or intrinsic). The problem here is that if the
changes in creatures do not affect God internally, or if God remains
ignorant of them on the model of relational change, then not only is
divine omnibenevolence threatened (in that God does not really care
about what happens to the creatures), so also is divine omniscience (in
that a being who was ignorant of what happened to the creatures would
not be the greatest knower).

Morris therefore offers a supplemental distinction, analogous to the
first, between relational change that occurs and relational change that
only appears to occur. Morris's view seems to be that only the latter applies
in the divine case: ". . . just as real change in one object can be reflected in
merely relational change in another, so real change with respect to God's
creatures can be reflected in the mere appearance of merely relational
change on the part of God" (Morris 1987, 134). God could not change
relationally if this entails ignorance, as in Morris's instructive example of
a woman who becomes a widow on the death of her husband, a death of
which she is unaware. This is in contrast to her being present at her husband's death, in which case she would undergo real change by becoming
a widow.

The implication here is an odd one: God is not altogether atempo-
ral, but God does not change, either. Of course everyone who thinks

through the logic of perfection wants to insist on divine immutability in *some* sense (contra what Rogers says about neoclassical theists, as we will see). Minimally, one wants to say that God is morally dependable. Further, one wants to say, in light of the ontological argument, that God's existence is necessary and that God always acts in the best way possible. But Morris is reluctant to follow the neoclassical theist all the way to dipolar theism, wherein God's permanent existence is contrasted with God's eminently changeable actuality.

The fear Morris has is that by accepting the existence-actuality distinction we would be led to say that God's actuality is *essentially related to* creatures, which, in turn, would lead to a denial of God's free act of creation *ex nihilo*:

... if every existent individual is essentially related to other existent objects, and God is a necessarily existent individual, there must of necessity exist objects distinct from God to which he is related. And further, since every object distinct from God must be dependent on him as creature to creator, it follows that a created world necessarily exists. God is necessarily a creator. But any property an individual has necessarily, he does not have freely. So it follows that God never was free with respect to whether he would create a world distinct from himself. (Morris 1987, 138–139)

I acknowledge that it comes as a shock to classical theists like Morris to hear that God *needs* a world. But the price to pay for not saying that God's relational pole (God's actuality) involves a divine need for creatures is even more costly and leads to an even greater shock. This price is nothing less than the compromising of divine omnibenevolence, the compromising of eminent divine love.

Consider the following statements:

A. X loves Y.
B. Y, who previously did not suffer, now starts to suffer.
C. In the face of Y's suffering, X remains unchanged.

Something is amiss. Indeed, the analogy between human love and divine love has been stretched to the breaking point. One can legitimately question whether X really loves Y, even assuming that X stands for God and Y stands for a creature. By refusing to consistently distinguish between the permanence of divine existence and the possibility that God could change (indeed, *must* change) in the divine actuality, Morris has left his view vulnerable to some of the most telling objections to classical theism, which skeptics like Rorty and Oppy assume are objections to theism itself.

It should be noted that some other philosophical theists deny classical theism, even the modified versions of it defended by Morris or
Alston, but nonetheless stop short of Hartshorne's neoclassical theism.
These "open theists" or "free will theists," who are often influenced by
Hartshorne, distinguish between the divine character as immutable and
specific divine experiences as changing. But they also, like Morris, defend
the doctrines of divine omnipotence and creation *ex nihilo*, doctrines
that create problems of their own (Pinnock 1994; cf., Viney 1998; Griffin
1991).

Another escape route is to adopt a muscular apophaticism (as in Mark
Taylor) by saying that God's love is nothing like human love. But there is a
stiff price to pay for this aggressive apophaticism, as we saw in Chapter 3.
Morris's own escape route is by way of a theological commitment to the
Christian doctrine of the trinity, which is conceived in terms of social relations among three divine persons. By arguing for social relations among
three divine persons, Morris hopes to show that divine reality is relational
within itself and at the same time to defend the claim that God does not
need the creatures. That is, there is no real change in God and only the
appearance of relational change with respect to the creatures. This view,
however, involves both a theological assumption regarding three divine
persons that cannot be philosophically proven and a lacunae regarding
how these divine persons can be related to the rest of reality if such relations are neither real nor relational.

I will say more later about the problems I see in Morris's view. Before
leaving him, however, I would like to note the second defect that he
sees in the neoclassical concept of God: that our immortality consists in
the events of our lives registering in the divine actuality. We live forever
in the mind of God. Morris thinks that this view is insufficient in that
he hopes to live forever in subjective immortality. On the view that he
identifies with neoclassical theism, however, God is ever changing by
actively registering in divine omniscience each new thing that happens.
This is the objective (not subjective) immortality of the past in the mind
of God. Even Morris admits the grandeur of this view, which militates
against the here today, gone tomorrow tenor of much contemporary life
(Morris 1987, 144–150).

In point of fact, neoclassical theists are divided on the issue of
immortality. The view that Morris identifies with neoclassical theism is
really Hartshorne's; Griffin, although a neoclassical theist, argues along
with Morris for subjective immortality of some sort (Griffin 2001); and
Whitehead was agnostic on the issue.

In the context of the present book, the problem with this part of Morris's critique, in which he argues for subjective immortality, is that not only does it signal a challenge to what is distinctively divine; it is also a trivialization of the ontological argument. The conclusion to the ontological argument is that *God* exists necessarily and hence is sovereign throughout all of time. To think that *we* should live forever in subjective immortality is hubris. What makes God distinctive is necessary existence and other perfections. By way of contrast, it should not surprise us to learn that as biological animals we have finite lifespans (Dombrowski 2004, 169–194).

The partial concessions that Morris makes to process theism are much like those of certain Thomists (Clarke 1979; Felt 2000) and of William Alston, whom I have criticized elsewhere (Alston 1984; Dombrowski 1994). By way of contrast, John Haldane is like a greater number of Thomists who are dismissive of *both* the ontological argument *and* process theism. In part the present book is meant to elicit a response from all of these parties regarding a contemporary neoclassical or process defense of the ontological argument. This is to be especially desired in the case of Haldane, whose Thomistic disdain for the ontological argument is such that he is willing to let the religious skeptic J. J. C. Smart state the (Oppy-like) case against the argument for him. Further, Haldane assumes, largely without argument, that the classical theistic version of the divine attributes is definitive (Haldane 1996, 38, 95, 145–147; 2004, 225).

Morris's "Anselmian explorations" lead him to make certain important concessions to the neoclassical use of the ontological argument, notably the ways in which neoclassical theists can render the argument more consistent with a dynamic biblical God who cares for the sufferings of creatures and more consistent with the dynamism of concepts in contemporary science. Katherin Rogers, however, in her view of "perfect being theology," makes no such concessions. She is a classical theist through and through. As a result, the problems with Morris's use of the ontological argument are magnified in Rogers' case. But Rogers is, unlike Haldane, nonetheless a defender of the ontological argument, and hence she deserves special attention.

Rogers is like many theists in seeing the medieval period as a golden age for philosophical theology. Even the Protestant reformers' concept of God largely consists in a return to Augustine, as David Ray Griffin has insightfully shown (Griffin 1989b, 109–145). From the perspective of neoclassical theism, this idealization of the medieval period is somewhat understandable in that the process view is as much neo*classical* as it is *neo*classical. Rogers pays little attention, however, to neoclassical critiques of classical theism, stating (inaccurately) only that the view of process thinkers is that God is not immutable and that God is "becoming better than He is" (Rogers 2000, 2–13; also Vaught 1972, 19; Hartt 1963). To be precise, we have seen that the necessary existence of God in the onto-logical argument makes it legitimate to defend the immutability of God's existence. Further, the logic of perfection leads us to say that God is *always* omnibenevolent such that God does not get better in the possession of this attribute. It is in divine actuality that God creatively advances and responds to the creative advances of others.

I would like to make it clear that I do not object to perfect being theology itself. Indeed, I think of myself as offering an alternative version of this position. Rogers is on the mark when she claims that "the reasons for believing that God must be a best possible or perfect being are closely related to the reasons for believing that there is a God at all" (Rogers 2000, 4–6). But the divine attributes she concludes to are those of the medieval thinkers. These attributes are accepted in a largely uncritical fashion: absolute independence of creatures, strict unity, unmitigated immutability, eternity rather than everlastingness, and so on.

Possible rapprochement with Rogers can be achieved via her defense of Anselmian libertarian freedom (in contrast, say, to Augustine's and Thomas' compatibilism). But this is a limited achievement when it is realized that it is unclear *how* human beings could be free given the divine attributes she defends, including divine knowledge – in minute detail and with absolute assurance – of what will happen to us in the future. In contrast to Morris, Rogers thinks that her conception of God as static is nonetheless compatible (but how?) with the dynamism exhibited by the biblical God (Rogers 2000, 9, 71–91).

Rogers defends a modal version of the ontological argument wherein God's essence is to exist necessarily. That is, God must exist in all possible worlds. My question is: what does it mean to be the greatest conceivable being, the perfect being? She claims, in partial agreement with Morris, that there only *seems* to be contingent truth in God. In short, to be tempo-ral *in any sense* is to be limited, on her view (Rogers 2000, 19–20, 32–38, 40–46, 54–55).

Premodern, Modern, Postmodern

Most of the difficulties with Morris's and Rogers' uses of the ontologi-cal argument arise from their view, borrowed from premodern classical

theism, that God is a supernatural, eternal, immutable being who creates the world *ex nihilo* by a free act of will. (This characterization fits
Rogers a bit more closely than it does Morris.) As is well known, this
supernaturalistic God was eventually seen in the late modern period to
be a fifth wheel in the effort to explain the world. Morris and especially
Rogers continue the premodern and early modern tendency to defend
a cosmological dualism wherein a supernatural (ghostly) God is seen as
hovering above the machine of the world which He (the male pronoun
seems appropriate here) made from nothing. Late modern atheists and
agnostics like Rorty and Oppy simply exorcise this ghost.

The omnipotent unilateralism of the God defended by Morris and
Rogers leads to standard questions in the philosophy of religion: how can
human beings be free if such a God already knows in minute detail and
with absolute assurance what they will do tomorrow?; or again, how can
human beings be free if divine *knowing* what they will do is also a divine
doing?; what is the point of spiritual discipline if God already knows (or
has predestined) whether we will be saved or damned?; if God is truly
*omni*potent, what power is left for us if the very act of existing involves at
least *some* power on our part to affect others or to be affected by others (a
la Plato)?; and so forth. Admittedly there is a long history of responding
to these and other questions, and I won't attempt to detail these responses
here. Rather, I wish to point out that it makes sense for Rorty, Taylor, and
Oppy to continue modern skepticism regarding the classical theistic concept of God. Fortunately, this view of God is not the only one, nor is it the
only one that is consistent with the ontological argument. There is a constructive (rather than deconstructive) postmodern alternative provided
by neoclassical theists (e.g., Griffin 1989b).

Divine and human actuality as well as divine and human power need
not be competitive, as classical theists imply (although admittedly classical theists would be reluctant to admit that there is such competition).
Loving cooperation between the two is not only logically possible, it is
a more fitting condition for divine actuality, given the logic of perfection, than the confused condition found in classical theism where God
is omnibenevolent and yet is unmoved by the creatures. At their best,
this is what classical theists intended: that divine grace did not destroy
human freedom and that contemplative union with God could be liberating rather than annihilating. But it is questionable whether classical
theists can explain how these worthy goals can be achieved on the terms
of their own theory. Traditional complaints by mystics of "the God of the
philosophers" (i.e., the God of the classical theists) are evidence of these
difficulties (Griffin 1989b, 109–125).

It should be emphasized that the supernaturalist classical theism defended by Morris and Rogers involves an extreme sort of voluntarism. Creation *ex nihilo*, which is not necessarily the biblical view of creation (Griffin 2001, 137–144), requires a God who is absolutely independent of creation and who is free to create or not to create it. It is quite understandable why Thomists might claim that their brand of theism has not usually been seen as voluntaristic. But Thomists are often voluntarists in spite of themselves in that the Thomistic version of classical theism has usually been used in the service of the voluntarist idea that a strictly independent, supernatural, eternal God can do exactly as He pleases (once again, the male pronoun seems appropriate here). This is odd given the tools within Thomism to resist voluntarism: the concepts of emanation and especially participation, the restriction on divine power provided by divine omnibenevolence, and so forth. As David Ray Griffin puts the point: "In spite of all that Thomas says about contingency, secondary causes, and freedom, a careful reading shows that everything happens just as it does because of God's primary causation" (Griffin 1989b, 130). To be precise, Thomas's affirmation of creation *ex nihilo* and of divine unilateralism come by way of revealed truth. It is noteworthy that on Thomistic (rather than on, say, Augustinian) grounds natural reason would have a difficult time establishing these positions.

As Griffin insightfully sees the matter, there are at least four characteristics that are essential to the classical theistic view of God, a view that is found in both Morris's (sometimes inconsistently) and Rogers' work:

1. The fact that the world exists, and the nature of the relations between it and God, are solely due to the omnipotent will of God.
2. God essentially has all the power; no power is inherent in the world and its members.
3. God can therefore exert unilateral, controlling power over the creatures.
4. If and when God loves the creatures, this is a free act; nothing prevents God's hating or being indifferent to the creatures (Griffin 1989b, 132).

It is because of the problems brought on by these characteristics that it is worth the effort to rethink the logic of perfection, most notably by thinking through the existence-actuality distinction, so as to have a more rationally defensible theism than that found in the work of classical theists like Morris and Rogers.

If Griffin is correct, as I think he is, that the basic religious motive is the *imitatio Dei*, then the concept of God defended by classical theists should be criticized. This is because a divine love that could exist indifferently with or without creatures bends the notion of love to the breaking point. Indeed, it leaves theism vulnerable to the most vicious aspects of the theodicy problem. Is genocide all that bothersome if the divine life is not much, if at all, affected by the loss (Griffin 1989b, 134)? Consider the following: Rogers thinks that an omnipotent and omnibenevolent God is compatible with the Holocaust (and presumably with the deaths of three million Poles) in that the Nazis only ruled for about twelve years, instead of the thousand-year rule planned for the Third Reich (Rogers 2000, 144). Even if Haught is correct that the theodicy problem is a difficult one to deal with no matter what one's theoretical commitments (Haught 2000, 55), the insufficiency of Rogers' sort of theodicy in particular is, as I see things, breathtaking.

Of course our particular world does not have to exist if creatures have some measure of freedom. But if actuality by its nature involves synthesizing past influences and deciding where to go next, it does not make much sense to talk about a time when there were no past influences, when God existed all alone. In a constructive postmodern, neoclassical, process theism a view is defended that is thoroughly naturalistic, as the following from Griffin indicates:

The existence of a world is, like God's own existence, fully natural or necessary.... God does not exist outside the universal order of causal interaction with the freedom to violate this order at will. Rather, the whole complex, God-and-a-world, exists naturally or necessarily, [along] with those basic principles that are called metaphysical because they could not be otherwise. These principles belong to the very nature of God and of the world, that is, of the total natural complex, God-and-a-world. (Griffin 1989b, 139–140)

It is my intention to argue for the superiority of this sort of appropriation of the logic of perfection to the sort defended by classical theists like Morris and Rogers.

The motto of the Jesuits (*ad majorem Dei gloriam*: all for the greater glory of God) could serve as a motto for theists in general. But on classical theistic assumptions, this motto makes little sense in that God's glory (in this context, God's actuality) cannot be greater than it is already in that God is not affected by our efforts at *imitatio Dei*. Assuming that we know as a result of the ontological argument that God exists necessarily, it is not really possible for us to remain indifferent to this knowledge, nor would it make sense for us to react negatively to it. That is, upon coming to the knowledge that God exists necessarily we can only respond in a positive way. But how could the greatest conceivable being remain unmoved by such a response, or be changed by such human knowers only relationally, if at all (Viney 1985, 29, 119–128)?

We saw earlier that once the contingency of God's existence drops out as a viable alternative, God's existence is either impossible or necessary. This is why getting a coherent concept of God is so important in that once we have such a coherent concept and can eliminate the impossibility of God's existence as a viable alternative, we can conclude that God exists necessarily. Admittedly the issue is complicated by the fact that the *conceivability* of God is different from the *coherence* of the concept of God in that conceivability is a psychological term, whereas coherence is a logical one. One can perhaps conceive of some things that are, due to our ignorance of internal contradictions in them, not really coherent (Steinitz 1994).

It is much harder, however, to conceive of something that has been shown to be incoherent. One strategy employed here by classical theists is to play with ad hoc devices so as to try to eliminate incoherence. Classical theists largely spend their exegetical and logical energy trying to extricate themselves from various types of incoherence in their view. To cite one more example (in addition to those mentioned above regarding the difficulty involved in reconciling divine omniscience with respect to the future and human freedom, or regarding the difficulty involved in reconciling divine love with the concept of an unmoved God who does not change), consider the famous challenge from Hume: how can evil exist in a world ruled by an omnipotent God who is also omnibenevolent?

It must be admitted that an improved view of God (conceivable and presumably coherent) will not sway some religious skeptics. Oppy, for example, thinks that debates regarding the concept of God are "unimportant." He fails to notice, however, that these debates have implications for the existence of God, an issue that he *does* recognize as important (Oppy 1996, 229).

David Pailin is one commentator who has seen clearly the connection between a neoclassical concept of God that is far more religiously appropriate than the classical concept, on the one hand, and defense of the ontological argument, on the other. As he puts it: "this distinction between the necessary existence and the contingent actuality of God is most important for understanding the ontological argument" (Pailin 1968, 107). To assume that God's perfection is *entirely* static is to assume that *all* change is for the worse. But if reality is not in a fixed state, we should intuitively see that not all change is for the worse, otherwise we would be left with a romantic *ur*-perfect world that gradually becomes attenuated. For example, "God, in order to have perfect knowledge, must grow in actual knowledge as each new event occurs and so becomes knowable as having occurred" (Pailin 1968, 108). Pailin also rightly notes that the neoclassical use of the ontological argument leads to a conclusion that is very abstract. This will disappoint some who want to obtain from the argument detailed knowledge of God's actuality, of what God is like in less abstract terms. But here we should remain (unless we have had religious experiences) agnostic. As Pailin puts the point:

This does not mean, as Hartshorne is concerned to point out, that God is the exception to all rational rules – for such an implication would make the concept of God simply nonsensical. What it does mean is that God is not subject to the rules appropriate only to contingent realities: he is subject to the truly universal rules that apply to all reality, necessary and contingent. (Pailin 1968, 119)

It is no small accomplishment to clarify, as the ontological argument does, the two abstract options available to us regarding the existence of God: the universe is either necessarily theistic or necessarily nontheistic.

The Noncompetitive and the Competitive

From what has been said thus far, we can conclude that there is nothing that can prevent God's existence. Hence it can be seen as noncompetitive. By way of contrast, God's actuality *is* competitive in the sense that the decisions of creatures are at least partly free in their type of response to the divine lure. Further, if God is also partly free regarding how exactly to respond to the creatures' responses (God *must* respond in an optimal way), some options will become actualized and others not. In classical theism, however, there is an absence on the part of God of any need or capacity to respond to creatures, hence God's reality is entirely noncompetitive. This leads to the neoclassical theist's worry that such a "God" does not really exhibit love or compassion (literally: feeling *with* others), but only offers an "as if" simulation of these. It would make more sense to say that the admission of divine accidents (competitive divine ways of responding to competitive creaturely responses to divine perfection) is obligatory (Hartshorne 1965, 66–67, 106–107). In this regard Viney is correct to point out that classical theism is really a type of theological behaviorism: God can act or *behave* lovingly, but God can have *no feelings* of love.

As long as one is talking about different aspects of deity, the law of noncontradiction is not violated by claiming that God is maximally independent regarding abstract properties like existence and maximally dependent regarding concrete properties like actual loving responses to the creatures' own responses to the divine lure. Both of these are perfections and hence do not contradict, but ideally conform to, the logic of perfection. Morris's (if not Rogers') concessions to neoclassical theism should have pushed him in this direction. If God is the greatest knower and lover, then there never could be an absence of a world to know and love, although not necessarily *this* world. To affirm that God is in some concrete state is not to say *how* God (or anyone else) is concrete; this affirmation itself is abstract (Hartshorne 1965, 122, 128–129, 301–302).

To be perfect is to be unsurpassable by another. This is the insight that is confusedly stated by Rogers as the process idea that God is becoming "better than He is." The point to the ontological argument is that God's existence does not compete with other possibilities if competitiveness is the very meaning of contingency. For example, our existence competes with our nonexistence at each moment. However, "the divine existence is not competitive and is the only noncompetitive or completely abstract (yet individual) existential role" (Hartshorne 1983, 100). We have seen that, on the classical theistic view, the existence of evil in the world might legitimately be seen as competing with the existence of an omnipotent God (although classical theists themselves tend not to see the competition here). This was an insightful contribution to philosophical theology made by Hume. The neoclassical view is one wherein God is seen as possessing maximal power that is compatible with the other divine attributes, especially omnibenevolence, but not as possessing *omni*potence if this means that other existents ultimately have no power of their own. That is, the neoclassical theist's God does not compete with evil for existence, as does the God of classical theism (Hartshorne 1983, 99–101).

If any claim is necessary, it would have to concern an abstract truth; if a claim is contingent, it concerns something concrete. In this regard, it seems that Kant was correct in suggesting that without a sensory intuition we cannot know an individual *in its concreteness*. Abstractly, however, we can know that God as unsurpassable has to be nonlocalized and ubiquitous; this is the optimal relation to space analogous to necessary existence throughout all of time. Because there are mutually contradictory examples of definiteness or concreteness, however, we cannot know via the ontological argument *how* God exists at any particular time in (real!) relation with a finite being at some particular place. Leibniz made the heroic effort to find an a priori reason for the particulars of the world; it should not escape our notice that he failed in this regard. In bare existence, God is not a particular nor is God concrete (Hartshorne 1970, 246–253).

Critics of the ontological argument need to tell us: what existential status, other than necessary existence, is compatible with perfection? Whereas defenders of the ontological argument who are classical theists need to tell us: can one give us on a classical theistic basis a consistent concept of God that avoids the inconsistencies mentioned in this chapter? It is easy to understand why some thinkers tire of trying to understand how God can help those in misery while not suffering sympathetically with them: "How can a being know what wretchedness is if no shadow of suffering, disappointment, unfulfilled desire or wish, has ever been experienced by that being?" (Hartshorne 2000, 104). There is no good reason to revive the ancient heresy of Patripassionism (the view that what befalls the Son – e.g., death – befalls the Father) if this position questions the continuation of God's existence. It is the divine actuality that suffers sympathetically with others (Hartshorne 2000, 96–106).

No doubt some classical theists like Rogers will say that, on neoclassical grounds, God's earlier actual state is inferior to later actual states. One snappy rejoinder to this criticism is to say that it involves an inferior concept of inferiority. If God always re-sponds to creatures' responses to the divine lure in the best way possible, it is inaccurate to say that earlier responses are "inferior." They were the best responses possible at that time. Indetermination comes with the (temporal) territory. And at each moment the immediately indeterminate becomes determinate as present decisions are made. Both potentiality and actuality characterize the divine being-in-becoming, as Morris at times implies. For example, God has the potential to love every sentient creature, but as omnibenevolent God loves creatures in their differences and hence responds to them differently. The greatest conceivable being-in-becoming would be characterized by modal coincidence: everything actual would be apprehended by divine knowing and everything potential would be appreciated as such, rather than appreciated as already actualized (Hartshorne 1962, vi, 3, 18, 35–38).

Anselm himself, for all his genius regarding how to argue for the existence of God, has a problematic classical theistic concept of God. For example, he follows Boethius in seeing God's interminable life as a perfect whole all at once outside of time. But what kind of *life* is this if life involves temporal progression and if temporal progression from moment to moment involves confrontation with at least a partially indeterminate future? (Anselm 1982, 51, 83; Hartshorne 1944, 228–231).

It is a mistake, I think, to assume that the temporal deity of neoclassical theism is unfit for the title of "greatest conceivable being." In the human case, not only are our actualities competitive, so also are our existences; although actual divine states are competitive, divine existence is noncompetitive. We can stay in existence only in certain environments, but God has the ability to exhibit eminent adaptability to every environment, and hence there is no beginning or ending to the divine existence. As before, there is no need to dogmatically assert that existence *has to be* contingent, or that an individual *has to interact* with others locally rather than cosmically (as a World Soul, say). The key is to avoid making either "necessity" or "contingency" into a theological fetish: both are required in a description of the divine nature that avoids the obvious defects in classical theism (Hartshorne 1967a, 39, 50, 124).

I do not believe in two gods. The formal and the material aspects of deity are separable intellectually, but they are inextricably tied together and mutually reinforce each other in reality (Wiehl 1991, 446). I agree with Whitehead's belief that our most abstract concepts provide our best tools for understanding concrete matters of fact and practical affairs *as a reticulative whole*. But understanding concrete matters of fact and practical affairs *in their particularity* is a different issue. Abstract concepts do not tell us what exactly will happen next in the creative advance of the universe and of the partially free beings in it (cf. Martin 1984). Divine actuality concerns the *how* of divine reality, whereas the ontological argument concerns merely the *somehow* or other (Hartshorne 1977, 162).

All can agree that the ontological argument is an exercise in metaphysics. But this latter term means different things to different thinkers. As I use the word, "metaphysics" refers to the philosophical study that tries to clarify our concepts of the necessary, the universal, the absolute, and the abstract. Clearly these terms are not synonymous, but there is a family resemblance among them that distinguishes them from their correlative opposites, which are in a different family: the contingent, the particular, the relative (or the relational), and the concrete, respectively. By contrasting these two sets of terms in this way, it can be seen that the denial of metaphysics consists in the (sometimes dogmatic) claim that everything is contingent, particular, relative, and concrete (Hartshorne 1961a, 107). On this basis, neither Morris nor Rogers is an opponent of metaphysics.

It does not make much sense to speak of a concrete, particular thing being necessary, given the indeterminacy involved in bringing that concrete particular into existence. It is a different matter when dealing with whole classes of contingent beings. In extensional language, the concept of contingent beings must be exemplified (but not any particular contingent thing) due to the utter unintelligibility of the "existence" of absolute nonbeing. *Something* exists. It is the class of contingent things in general that cannot be empty. Connected with this is the idea that, if contingent things that exist have to be related to other things that exist, there is a sort of absoluteness to relativity, contra Morris and Rogers. In the divine case this means that God is perfectly related at all times to all concrete particulars (Hartshorne 1961a, 108–109).

Likewise, God's permanence consists in the fact that deity *always* changes. What is being challenged in the ontological argument is the hegemony of ordinary (contingent) existential statements. And what I am challenging in Morris's and Rogers' uses of the ontological argument is the eschewal of the distinction (more bothersome in Rogers' case) between divine existence and divine actuality.

We have seen that contingency can be characterized as the exclusion of certain existential possibilities, whereas necessity is noncompetitive with such possibilities. Or again:

There are, then, three modal forms of existential statement: those which contradict every positive existential assertion; those which contradict some positive existential assertions but agree with others; those which contradict no such assertions. (Hartshorne 1961a, 111)

These three forms of statement deal with the impossible, the empirical, and the metaphysical, respectively. To claim that "God's existence is necessary" is a metaphysical statement is to say something that is compatible with the claim that "God's actuality is not necessary" if the details of God's necessary existence are open to various factors. The stumbling block here for Morris and Rogers seems to lie in the assumption that "ideal power" is synonymous with "monopoly of power" over all the details of the universe, including divine actuality. There is no defect in God in sharing the world with others, however.

A perfect God is compatible with an imperfect world only if there is a multiplicity of partly self-determining creatures whose decisions have the possibility of conflicting with each other. It is only on the classical theistic assumptions of Morris and Rogers that the presence of evil in the world becomes a real cipher: how could evil possibly exist? Concreteness as such is necessary, but not any particular concrete acts, which depend at least in part on creaturely decisions. As a result of the neoclassical view of God, the key objection to the ontological argument (reiterated in different ways by Rorty, Taylor, and Oppy) is removed: the concrete is *not* derived from an abstract definition. The abstract modality of God's noncompetitive existence is treated in the argument, not the concrete and competitive modality of God's actuality (Hartshorne 1961a, 112–121).

One thing I hope to achieve with this book is to direct attention away from the differences between contemporary analytic philosophy of religion and the apophaticism in contemporary continental philosophy of religion. The more telling difference is between the classical theistic assumptions often found in both analytic and continental circles, on the one hand, and neoclassical theism, on the other. Neoclassical theism abandons the classical theistic assumption that God is *purely* necessary. That is, we should indeed pay a debt to Anselm, but it is nonetheless possible to be too Anselmian.

Plantinga and *Aseity*

Despite Plantinga's enormous contribution to the defense of the ontological argument, in particular, and regarding the metaphysics of modality, in general (Plantinga 1974; 2003) – especially his defense of *de re* modality against Quine and his use of a temporal analogy to understand transworld identity – he remains a classical theist with respect to his concept of God. Perhaps it will be claimed that, although Plantinga has assumed, rather than defended, strict divine immutability and omnipotence, there are nonetheless good reasons for such assumptions because, say, if God were not immutable God's *aseity* would be compromised. Plantinga notes that two demands of the "religious attitude" are that God exists necessarily and that God should possess "various qualities in some necessary manner" (Plantinga 1967, 78, 174–180). I agree with Plantinga here, at least if one of these qualities is the ability always to respond to the momentary sufferings of creatures (n.b., "always" *and* "respond"). But from this demand that God's character be *a se*, Plantinga emphasizes the necessary absence of certain kinds of change in God.

It might seem that Plantinga is not as committed to divine immutability as Morris and especially Rogers in that he says that it is "surely clear" that God does undergo change, as in the change from not being worshipped by St. Paul in 100 BCE to being so worshipped in 40 CE. But this change for Plantinga is a relational or logical one (more precisely, an external relation). God's eternal being, he thinks, is not merely changeless but unchangeable. He sides with St. Augustine in denying the distinction between divine necessary existence (that God exists) and divine

contingent actuality (how God exists). That is, he denies dipolarity in God
(Plantinga 1967). The reason Plantinga sides with the classical theistic
tradition is that there is an essential connection, as he sees it, between
divine *aseity* ("his uncreatedness, self-sufficiency, and independence of
everything else") and omnipotence (his control over all things). Plantinga
frequently refers to God as omnipotent. It is clear that Plantinga is familiar with Hartshorne's work on the ontological argument, but it is not
clear that he is interested in, or even familiar with, neoclassical theism
(Plantinga 1974).

I also agree with Plantinga that God does not depend on us for divine
existence, nor does God depend on us in particular for omnibenevolence. But, if not us in particular, then some creatures or other would
be needed for God to know and love in order for God to have the properties of omniscience and omnibenevolence. This divine dependence is
more than what Plantinga would claim is "Pickwickian." To claim rightly,
as Plantinga does, that even the religious rebel's existence is dependent
on God does not establish, as he thinks, that the rebel has no significant
effect on God (Plantinga 1980, 2–3).

For various reasons, Plantinga does not defend divine simplicity, but
this denial also, he thinks, poses a threat to divine *aseity* because if abstract
objects of a Platonic sort are different from God's nature they threaten
not only divine simplicity, but also the notion of divine control. But it
is important to notice that Plantinga himself admits that *his* notion of
sovereignty-*aseity* is (merely) an intuition (Plantinga 1980, 34, 68).

There are, at the very least, plausible grounds for believing that abstract
objects do not threaten God's *aseity*, hence do not conflict with the denial
of immutability in the divine actuality. That is, one can criticize immutability with respect to divine actuality, still preserve *aseity* with respect to divine
existence, as well as allow for the sorts of abstract objects with which
Plantinga is concerned. "X is independent of Y" minimally implies that
it could be the case that X exists while Y does not, which implies that
Y is contingent. If X stands for abstract objects and Y for God, then the
nonexistence of God is being taken as possible. But this "possibility" conflicts with Plantinga's own defense of the ontological argument (albeit
in reformed epistemology fashion: although one cannot *prove* that God
exists through the ontological argument, one can show that it is rational to
accept theism on the basis of this argument). If one asks whether abstract
objects have supremacy over God, one should respond that the issue is
secondary and largely verbal because both abstract objects and God are

everlasting and independence has no clear meaning between everlasting things. Abstract objects are those that would always be understood by an omniscient God (Hartshorne 2000, 56–57).

Plantinga assumes that God could not be embodied in any sense; he thinks that theists have always held that God is immaterial. Because if God were material God would change, there is no apparent need to argue any further for divine immateriality. But on historical grounds Plantinga is in trouble here. David of Dinant and Hobbes are not, as he thinks, the only philosophers who have defended divine embodiment. As Plutarch attests, almost all of the ancient philosophers, including Plato, believed in God as the World Soul who animates the body of the world. This view positively affected Origen. These examples, along with Hartshorne's life-long defense of the Platonic World Soul, are noteworthy omissions in Plantinga's historical gloss (Dombrowski 1991; 2005). My point here is to notice the intellectual and historical thinness of Plantinga's assumption that God must be completely immaterial, in order that he might preserve belief in strict divine *aseity*. The distinction between existence and actuality would help him to see that divine *aseity* of existence is not threatened by the doctrine of God as the World Soul (Jantzen 1984; Clayton and Peacocke 2004).

Admittedly Plantinga thinks that God's "eternity" is not timeless, but rather consists in endless and beginningless duration. Or better, it consists in sempiternity or everlastingness, hence in this regard Plantinga is a bit like Morris and unlike Rogers. From this belief, however, Plantinga does not make the understandable move toward neoclassical theism, but (like Morris) tries to hold on to the classical theistic belief in a God whose knowledge is not "temporally limited" (Plantinga 1980, 45). God, for Plantinga, right now knows even the remote future in minute detail, but God is not timeless (whatever this means!). God in some peculiar way acts in time and does some things before others, he thinks, but God is not affected by time or change (Plantinga 1980, 45–46).

Plantinga has a very strong sense of God as absolutely omnipotent (Plantinga 1974; 1980), of God in control of everything, or, as Hartshorne would put it in a way that very often angers classical theists, of God as despot. We should agree with Plantinga that the notion of God as maximal power is "non-negotiable" from the perspective of theism (Plantinga 1980, 134), but what it means to have maximal power is a matter of disagreement. *Omni*potence in the classical theistic sense of the term conflicts with belief in human freedom, and the statistical nature of scientific

laws (as in Peirce), and creates the nastiest version of the theodicy problem. The point I want to make here, again, however, is that neoclassical
theists have spent a great deal of energy criticizing in detail the concept of
omnipotence and analytic theists like Morris, and especially Rogers and
Plantinga, have not paid sufficient attention to these critiques. Moreover,
the unquestioned assumption that immutability is integral to what neoclassical theists call divine actuality is connected to Plantinga's overly
strong view of divine omnipotence. For, in his view, if God were not
omnipotent He (the male pronoun is needed here) would not be in
control and could be pushed around (that is, changed) by others.

The Religious Significance of the Ontological Argument

Nothing in this book is meant to suggest that the soundness of the ontological argument is the only question to be raised regarding the existence
of God. There are also the concrete religious experiences claimed by various people (and the sort of intelligibility they lend to the coherence of
the concept of God) and the other arguments for the existence of God.
That is, along with Morris, Rogers, and Plantinga we should note the
experiential and religious setting within which reflection on the ontological argument takes place. Anselm himself thought it consistent to
philosophize while praying. In this regard the following point should be
emphasized: the ontological argument from the time of Anselm to the
present has always been involved in *both* assimilation of religious experience and tradition *and* refinement of our concept of what it means to be
the greatest conceivable being. The neoclassical version of perfect being
theology simply continues this history of conservation and modification
(Smith 1968, 121–124; Schrimpf 1994).

Neither a theistic argument without the support of religious experience nor a religious experience without theoretical support is a desirable
state of affairs. We do not need discursive arguments regarding the existence of ordinary objects; we just put ourselves in the presence of the
objects. But in the case of God we do not know what it would be like to
be in the presence of God via ordinary experience. However, extraordi-
nary (albeit natural) experiences of God have been recorded throughout human history and across various cultures. It is not the case that a
defender of the ontological argument needs to conclude to the existence
of God as a result of either having a religious experience or reading about
others who have claimed to have had them. These experiences can be
seen as establishing only that the concept of God is coherent, at least

if we assume that the object of these experiences can be identified with the God of the ontological argument. This possibility *when harnessed to the ontological argument* shows that God must exist. As before, God's existence could not be contingent, but must be either impossible or necessary (Smith 1968, 125–127).

John Smith is instructive regarding the pragmatist version of the key objection to the ontological argument articulated in different ways by Rorty, Taylor, and Oppy: the ontological argument provides us with a *rational* encounter with the necessary existence of God, but not with an *actual* encounter in experience. Smith himself points the way toward an adequate, twofold response to this objection. First, a rational encounter *is* an experience of a certain sort. There is no reason why religious thinking and religious experience in general have to be seen as belonging to two different ontological realms. Although Morris, Rogers, and Plantinga are defenders of the ontological argument, they nonetheless encourage this sort of dualism by placing God in a supernatural realm outside of this world. Second, Smith is well aware of the fact that the neoclassical version of the ontological argument, for which he has a certain grudging admiration, does not move from the abstract concept of God to the concrete actuality of God, as is often assumed (Smith 1968, 128).

The point to be learned from Smith's pragmatism is that a defense of the ontological argument should be seen as a moment in the life of a reasonable human being seeking intelligibility; the *telos* of this intelligibility is to approximate the truth ever more closely and hence to live better. A neoclassical version of the ontological argument indeed helps us to think better, but this does not mean that the argument is intended to be a knockdown proof that carries an unwilling thinker along with it. Rather, the ontological argument provides a religious believer with rational support and it is a burr in the saddle of those who treat claims to religious experience with utter contempt. For example, it pushes a religious skeptic like Oppy away from atheism and toward agnosticism. In neither case, however, is it dialectically worthless (Smith 1968, 129–133).

Smith is also instructive in a more recent essay regarding neoclassical theism's achievements in light of the entire history of the ontological argument. Three points should be highlighted. First, he notes that in Hartshorne's version of the argument divine existence is treated in an abstract way, in contrast to divine actuality. We have seen that this treatment enables us to avoid many of the traditional criticisms of the argument reiterated by contemporary critics like Rorty, Taylor, and

Oppy. Second, Smith recognizes that the neoclassical use of the ontological argument improves on Kant by connecting modality to the concept of God. By severing these two, Kant made it too easy to discredit
the argument. And third, Smith sees Hartshorne reversing the burden
of proof regarding the ontological argument. Rather than the defenders
of the argument being defens*ive* by virtue of their location in the pris-
oner's dock, they are now analogous to prosecuting attorneys, asking of
religious skeptics like Rorty, Taylor, and Oppy, what exactly is there about
the concept of God that makes the existence of such a being impossible
(Smith 1984, 103–104)?

A religious experience (frequently called a mystical experience) is
often characterized by scholars in terms of two features: an immediate
experience of God and of ineffability. Regarding the first characteristic
we should note how odd it would be to experience a being who was temporally everlasting and spatially ubiquitous only on the basis of indirect
evidence. That is, if the most readily detectable data are those that are
sometimes present and sometimes not (as in a sharp pain, a bright color,
or a large carnivore), this does not mean that it is impossible to detect
data that are everlasting and ubiquitous. The mystic can be seen as the
person who is consciously aware of directly experiencing what we all (at
least implicitly) experience indirectly: divine life (Dombrowski 1992).

Further, a neoclassical defense of the ontological argument is compatible as well with the second characteristic of religious experience. The
necessity of divine existence need not transcend language in that such
necessity is very abstract and, as we have seen, amenable to literal or near
literal discourse. The discourse about divine actuality, however, we have
seen to be anything but literal. What it is like to *be* God from moment
to moment at a concrete level can only be described in analogical or
symbolic language, at best. The difficulties involved in finding the right
analogy or the appropriate symbol to describe divine actuality can understandably lead one to say that such an actuality is, in a way, ineffable.
This does not mean that the effort to talk about divine actuality is point-
less, especially when it is considered that some analogies and symbols are
more misleading than others, as when classical theists use the symbol of
an unmoved mover to describe God (something like a Grand Magnet that
moves all the metal filings of the world, but that is not moved by them).
As Hartshorne puts the point: "Possibly we need to devote more time to
meditation and less (though at present it is no vast amount) to rationalistic metaphysics" (Hartshorne 1976, 469). That is, religious experience
might help us to develop better metaphors.

Rogers obviously thinks that her classical theistic view of God, which does not make the distinction between divine existence and divine actuality, is superior to the neoclassical view. James Ross, by way of contrast, thinks that there is a stalemate between the two views such that it is difficult to decide between them (Ross 1977). Smith, however, encourages neoclassical theists to go on the offensive by pressing their cases regarding both the necessary existence and contingent actuality of God on religious skeptics and classical theists, respectively. It is by no means clear that Rogers' view trumps religious skepticism and neoclassical theism merely because classical theism has historically been the dominant stance; presumably Morris's doubts about classical theism and his concessions to neoclassical theism are evidence of the strength of Smith's stance here.

It is true that Smith is not entirely convinced that defenders of the ontological argument, whether they be classical theists or neoclassical theists, have overcome the objection that necessity is always *de dictu*. The reason why he is nonetheless fascinated with the ontological argument, and especially with the neoclassical version of it, and thinks that it is hardly worthless, is that on the basis of this argument the nonexistence of God is appropriately seen as contradictory. Rorty, Taylor, and Oppy are typical of those with nominalist tendencies who "blithely" reject the argument. We have seen in Oppy's case that by implicitly adopting nominalism he has paid quite a philosophic price for rejecting the ontological argument. Smith's pragmatism leads him to be a bit more thrifty (Smith 1984, 105–108).

If faith in God is a real possibility in the sense that it would not commit one to logical inconsistencies, then utter refutation of the ontological argument is going to be extraordinarily difficult. Oppy (as an agnostic) admits as much. Further, the neoclassical recovery of *life* within the divine nature helps, Smith thinks, in averting the standard inconsistencies found within classical theism (Smith 1984, 109).

Philip Devine, in an article with the same title as this section of the chapter, notes that the various sorts of belief and doubt regarding the existence of God do not seem to indicate that we are dealing with a demonstrable truth. But we might nonetheless be dealing with one in that the disagreements very often concern something that the argument does not show: that the concept of God is coherent. And this possibility is required in order to push the argument through. However, the dialectical worth of the argument surfaces not only in the way in which it can help to clarify theistic belief, but also in the way in which it complicates matters for the religious skeptic, who must now show why the existence of God is impossible; the skeptic cannot retreat to the (Humean) option that suggests that God's existence is contingent (Devine 1975b).

Anselm himself clearly intends the argument to be part of a larger, dialectical conversation. His *Monologion* is, in fact, a soliloquy or monologue, but the *Proslogion* is presented explicitly as a *discourse*. That is, the ontological argument, whether it is defended by Anselm, Morris, Rogers, Plantinga, Hartshorne, or myself, is an instance of faith seeking understanding. This understanding is currently sought in dialectical context with believers and unbelievers alike. Along with Anselm, however, I agree that *rational* understanding of God's existence is most valuable (Anselm 1982, 1–7, 159, 162, 178, 242).

My purpose here is both to explore the religious significance of the ontological argument and to indicate the religious superiority of the neoclassical version of the ontological argument to the classical version. It is *not* to claim that the religious significance of the argument overwhelms its rational significance, even to the point where it is no longer seen as an argument, but rather as a prayer. This effort would indeed, as Oppy rightly insists, be an obvious example of begging the question (Moore 2003; McGill 1967; cf. Stolz 1967; Barth 1960).

As Alexandre Koyre and others have correctly noted, Anselm, unlike contemporary defenders of the ontological argument, was arguing exclusively with believers. But at least one issue remains the same: then as now there is no experiential meaning for the nonexistence of God. The question is: is there experiential meaning for the existence of God? ("Experience" here is not to be confused with the term "empirical" as it was used by the British empiricists; the former is a much wider term than the latter.) The reports of the mystics in the Abrahamic and other religions encourage us to respond to this question in the affirmative (Koyre 1923; Hartshorne 1965, 53, 64–65).

There is no need for a defender of the ontological argument to deny the claim that we could hardly seek unless we had already (in some sense) found. This is because the ontological argument does not assume at the outset the existence of God, only a coherent concept of God. But such a coherent concept is unlikely in the classical theistic worldview found in Morris, Rogers, and Plantinga. Nor need one deny that the finding is at a lesser degree of clarity than is hoped for in the search. This is because the concrete details and the scope of divine actuality are largely beyond our grasp (Hartshorne 1941, 18–19, 59–60, 75–76, 312; 1944, 235–236).

There is much to be said in favor of the idea that objectivity is not to be found in any one thinker or in any one thinker's argument, but in the process of mutual inspiration and correction among several thinkers. The distinction between divine existence and divine actuality implies the mutual inspiration and correction supplied by the rationalists and the empiricists (or better, the pragmatists), respectively. Or again, there is something to be learned from those who see in God permanent being, but also from those who interpret the famous tetragrammaton of Exodus 3:14 in process terms. Neither ontolatry (worship of being) nor gignolatry (worship of becoming) should be defended in isolation from the other. Religious experience itself balks at the idea of a God who is *purely* static and who is not really related to the believer (Hartshorne 1962, viii–ix, 4, 8–9, 81–82, 111, 113, 116).

It is not my purpose here to explore the extent to which the ontological argument has religious significance outside of the Abrahamic religions. I would not want to close off such possibilities, however. To take just a few examples: the Taoist principle that the Tao is the supreme reality and is noncompetitive with contingent possibilities seems to show some resemblance to the noncompetitive nature of divine existence found as a result of the ontological argument; likewise regarding the "undying" and "ungenerated" as found in certain forms of Buddhism and in the strictly universal existence of the "sun" (God) in the ancient Egyptian figure Ikhnaton. I have only scratched the surface of what could be said here. It should not surprise us that, if the ontological argument is sound, religious thinkers from other traditions would have discovered something analogous in their own traditions (Hartshorne 1965, 146–148; Berthrong 1998; Clark 1990, 159; Mukerji 2001; Pruss 2001; Ghosh 1994).

In many parts of both the West and East, however, religious (including theistic) belief is in decline. This is due, in part, to defects in the ways that theists themselves have characterized ultimate reality. Human beings, along with nature, abhor a vacuum, such that "when the gods go the half-gods arrive" (Hartshorne 1948, 148–149). Not least among these are the worship of human power, language, and cleverness. Regarding religious skepticism one can easily understand the following sharp yet conciliatory remarks from Hartshorne:

Belief is a privilege. To scold or think ill of those who are unable or refuse to avail themselves of this privilege is inappropriate. To persecute them is monstrous. But there is also little need to congratulate them. Nor perhaps are they wise to congratulate themselves. (Hartshorne 1970, 297)

In addition to engaging in dialectical conversation with religious skeptics like Rorty, Taylor, and Oppy, it is also crucial to engage classical theists like Morris, Rogers, and Plantinga. In my own "Anselmian explorations" and "perfect being theology," respectively, I have come to the conclusion that otherworldliness, belief in unqualified divine immutability, and worship of unilateral, coercive divine power are among the half-gods.

Bibliography

Adams, R. M. 1994. *Leibniz: Determinist, Theist, Idealist.* New York: Oxford University Press.

Alston, William. 1984. "Hartshorne and Aquinas: A Via Media." In John Cobb, ed. *Existence and Actuality: Conversations with Charles Hartshorne.* Chicago: University of Chicago Press.

Altizer, Thomas. 1977. *The Self-Embodiment of God.* New York: Harper and Row.

Anderson, C. Anthony. 1990. "Some Emendations of Godel's Ontological Proof." *Faith and Philosophy* 7: 291–303.

Anselm, St. 1982. *Basic Writings.* S. N. Deane, tr. LaSalle, Illinois: Open Court.

Baird, Forrest. 1995. "A Simple Version of Anselm's Argument." *Teaching Philosophy* 18: 245–249.

Barnes, Jonathan. 1972. *The Ontological Argument.* London: Macmillan.

Barth, Karl. 1960. *Anselm: Fides Quaerens Intellectum.* Ian Robertson, tr. London: SCM Press.

Beckaert, A. 1967. "A Platonic Justification for the Argument *A Priori*." In John Hick, ed. *The Many-Faced Argument: Recent Studies on the Ontological Argument for the Existence of God.* New York: Macmillan.

Berthrong, John. 1998. *Concerning Creativity: A Comparison of Chu Hsi, Whitehead, and Neville.* Albany: State University of New York Press.

Brecher, Robert. 1985. *Anselm's Argument: The Logic of Divine Existence.* Aldershot, UK: Gower.

Burgess-Jackson, Keith. 1994. "Anselm, Gaunilo, and the Lost Island." *Philosophy and Theology* 8: 243–249.

Cargile, James. 1975. "The Ontological Argument." *Philosophy* 50: 69–80.

Ceniza, Claro. 2003. "Parmenides' Ontological Argument." *Philosophia* 32: 184–190.

Chambers, Timothy. 2000. "On Behalf of the Devil: A Parody of Anselm Revisited." *Proceedings of the Aristotelian Society* 100: 93–113.

Chappell, V. C. 1963. "Comment." In Ernan McMullin, ed. *The Concept of Matter.* Notre Dame: Notre Dame University Press.

Charlesworth, M. J. 1965. *St. Anselm's Proslogion.* Oxford: Clarendon Press.

Clark, Stephen. 1990. *A Parliament of Souls.* Oxford: Clarendon Press.

Clarke,W. Norris. 1979. *The Philosophical Approach to God.* Winston-Salem: Wake Forest University Press.

Clayton, Philip, and Arthur Peacocke, eds. 2004. *In Whom We Live and Move and Have Our Being.* Grand Rapids: Eerdmans.

Collins, James. 1954. *A History of Modern Philosophy.* Milwaukee: Bruce Publishing.

Cornman, James, Keith Lehrer, and George Pappas. 1987. "An *A Priori* Argument." In *Philosophical Problems and Arguments.* Indianapolis: Hackett.

Daniels, P. A. 1909. *Quellenbeitrage und Untersuchungen zur Geschichte der Gottesbeweise im XIII Jahrhundert, mit besonderer Beruchsichtigung des Arguments im Proslogion des Hlg. Anselm.* Munster: Beitrage zur Geschichte der Philosophie des Mitteralters.

Davies, Brian. 1985. "The Existence of God and the Concept of God." In *Thinking About God.* London: Geoffrey Chapman.

Davis, Stephen. 2003. "The Ontological Argument." In Paul Copan, ed. *The Rationality of Theism.* New York: Routledge.

Dennett, Daniel. 2000. "The Case for Rorts." In Robert Brandom, ed. *Rorty and His Critics.* Oxford: Blackwell.

Desmond, William. 2003. *Hegel's God: A Counterfeit Double?* Burlington, Vermont: Ashgate.

Devine, Philip. 1975a. "The Perfect Island, the Devil, and Existent Unicorns." *American Philosophical Quarterly* 12: 255–260.

———. 1975b. "The Religious Significance of the Ontological Argument." *Religious Studies* 11: 97–116.

———. 1975c. "Does St. Anselm Beg the Question?" *Philosophy* 50: 271–281.

Dombrowski, Daniel. 1983. "Rorty on Pre-Linguistic Awareness in Pigs." *Ethics & Animals* 4: 2–5.

———. 1988a. "Rorty on Plato as an Edifier." In Peter Hare, ed. *Doing Philosophy Historically.* Buffalo: Prometheus Books.

———. 1988b. *Hartshorne and the Metaphysics of Animal Rights.* Albany: State University of New York Press.

———. 1988c. "Does God Have a Body?" *Journal of Speculative Philosophy* 2: 225–232.

———. 1991. "Hartshorne and Plato." In Lewis Hahn, ed. *The Philosophy of Charles Hartshorne.* LaSalle, Illinois: Open Court.

———. 1992. *St. John of the Cross: An Appreciation.* Albany: State University of New York Press.

———. 1994. "Alston and Hartshorne on the Concept of God." *International Journal for Philosophy of Religion* 36: 129–146.

———. 1996a. "Hartshorne and Heidegger." *Process Studies* 25: 19–33.

———. 1996b. *Analytic Theism, Hartshorne, and the Concept of God.* Albany: State University of New York Press.

———. 1997. "Process Thought and the Liberalism-Communitarianism Debate: A Comparison with Rawls." *Process Studies* 26: 15–32.

———. 2001a. *Rawls and Religion: The Case for Political Liberalism.* Albany: State University of New York Press.

———. 2001b. "Charles Hartshorne." *Stanford Encyclopedia of Philosophy* (July 26). http://plato.stanford.edu.

———. 2004. *Divine Beauty: The Aesthetics of Charles Hartshorne*. Nashville: Vanderbilt University Press.

———. 2005. *A Platonic Philosophy of Religion: A Process Perspective*. Albany: State University of New York Press.

Dougherty, M. V. 2002. "The Importance of Cartesian Triangles: A New Look at Descartes' Ontological Argument." *International Journal of Philosophical Studies* 10: 35–62.

Downey, James. 1986. "A Primordial Reply to Modern Gaunilos." *Religious Studies* 22: 41–49.

Ellis, John. 1989. *Against Deconstruction*. Princeton: Princeton University Press.

Engel, Mylan. 1997. "The Possibility of Maximal Greatness Examined: A Critique of Plantinga's Modal Ontological Argument." *Acta Analytica*: 117–128.

Eslick, Leonard. 1982. "Plato's Dialectic of the Sun." In Linus Thro, ed. *History of Philosophy in the Making*. Washington, DC: University Press of America.

Esser, Mattias. 1905. *Der ontologische Gottesbeweis und seine Geschichte*. Bonn: Buchdruckerei von Seb. Foppen.

Everitt, Nicholas. 1995. "Kant's Discussion of the Ontological Argument." *Kant Studien* 86: 385–405.

———. 2004. *The Non-Existence of God*. New York: Routledge.

Felt, James. 2000. *Coming To Be: Toward a Thomistic-Whiteheadian Metaphysics of Becoming*. Albany: State University of New York Press.

Feuerbach, Ludwig. 1957. *The Essence of Christianity*. George Eliot, tr. New York: Harper and Row.

Findlay, J. N. 1948. "Can God's Existence Be Disproved?" *Mind* 57: 176–183.

Ford, Lewis, ed. 1973. *Two Process Philosophers*. Tallahassee: American Academy of Religion.

Forgie, William. 1972. "Frege's Objection to the Ontological Argument." *Nous* 6: 251–263.

Friedman, Joel. 1980. "Necessity and the Ontological Argument." *Erkenntnis* 15: 301–331.

Gale, Richard. 1998. "Review of Graham Oppy, *Ontological Arguments and Belief in God*." *Philosophy and Phenomenological Research* 58: 715–719.

Gettings, Michael. 1999. "Godel's Ontological Argument: A Reply to Oppy." *Analysis* 59: 309–313.

Ghosh, Raghunath. 1994. "Can There Be an Ontological Argument in Nyaya Vaisesika?" *Indian Philosophical Quarterly* 21: 119–127.

Gilson, Etienne. 1955. *History of Christian Philosophy in the Middle Ages*. New York: Random House.

Godel, Kurt. 1995. *Collected Works*. Vol. 3. New York: Oxford University Press.

Goodwin, George. 1978. *The Ontological Argument of Charles Hartshorne*. Missoula: Scholars Press.

———. 1983. "The Ontological Argument in Neoclassical Context: Reply to Friedman." *Erkenntnis* 20: 219–232.

———. 2003. "*De Re* Modality and the Ontological Argument." In George Shields, ed. *Process and Analysis*. Albany: State University of New York Press.

Grant, C. K. 1957. "The Ontological Disproof of the Devil." *Analysis* 17: 71–72.

Griffin, David Ray. 1976. *God, Power, and Evil: A Process Theodicy*. Philadelphia: Westminster Press.

———. 1989a. *The Varieties of Postmodern Theology*. Albany: State University of New York Press.

———. 1989b. *God and Religion in the Postmodern World*. Albany: State University of New York Press.

———. 1991. *Evil Revisited*. Albany: State University of New York Press.

———. 2001. *Reenchantment without Supernaturalism: A Process Philosophy of Religion*. Ithaca: Cornell University Press.

Haight, David, and Marjorie Haight. 1970. "An Ontological Argument for the Devil." *Monist* 54: 218–220.

Haldane, John. 1996. *Atheism and Theism*. Oxford: Blackwell.

———. 2004. *Faithful Reason: Essays Catholic and Philosophical*. London: Routledge.

Halfwassen, Jens. 2002. "Sein als uneingeschrankte Fulle: Zur Vorgeschichte des ontologischen Gottesbeweises im antiken Platonismus." *Zeitschrift fuer philosophische Forschung* 56: 497–516.

Hall, David. 2004. "Whitehead, Rorty, and the Return of the Exiled Poets." In Janusz Polanowski, ed. *Whitehead's Philosophy: Points of Connection*. Albany: State University of New York Press.

Hardy, James. 1996. "Burdens of Proof: Why Modal Ontological Arguments Aren't Convincing." *Journal of Philosophical Research* 21: 321–330.

Hare, R. M. 1981. "Nothing Matters." In E. D. Klemke, ed. *The Meaning of Life*. New York: Oxford University Press.

Harrison, Craig. 1970. "The Ontological Argument in Modal Logic." *Monist* 54: 302–313.

Hartshorne, Charles. 1923. An Outline and Defense of the Argument for the Unity of Being in the Absolute or Divine Good. Ph.D. dissertation. Harvard University.

———. 1929. "Review of *Sein und Zeit*." *Philosophical Review* 38: 284–293.

———. 1934. *The Philosophy and Psychology of Sensation*. Chicago: University of Chicago Press.

———. 1936. "The Compound Individual." In Otis Lee, ed. *Philosophical Essays for Alfred North Whitehead*. New York: Longmans Green.

———. 1939. "Are All Propositions About the Future Either True or False?" *Program of the American Philosophical Association: Western Division* (April 20–22): 26–32.

———. 1941. *Man's Vision of God*. New York: Harper and Row.

———. 1944. "The Formal Validity and Real Significance of the Ontological Argument." *Philosophical Review* 53: 225–245.

———. 1948. *The Divine Relativity*. New Haven: Yale University Press.

———. 1950. "The Divine Relativity and Absoluteness: A Reply." *Review of Metaphysics* 4: 31–60.

———. 1953. *Reality as Social Process*. Boston: Free Press.

———. 1955. "Process as Inclusive Category." *Journal of Philosophy* 52 (Feb. 17): 94–102.

————. 1961a. "Metaphysics and the Modality of Existential Judgments." In Ivor Leclerc, ed. *The Relevance of Whitehead*. New York: Macmillan.

————. 1961b. "The Logic of the Ontological Argument." *Journal of Philosophy* 58 (Aug. 17): 471–473.

————. 1962. *The Logic of Perfection*. LaSalle, Illinois: Open Court.

————. 1963a. "Real Possibility." *Journal of Philosophy* 60 (Oct. 10): 593–605.

————. 1963b. "Abstract and Concrete in God: A Reply." *Review of Metaphysics* 17: 289–295.

————. 1964. "Replies to 'Interrogations of Charles Hartshorne, Conducted by William Alston'." In Sydney Rome, ed. *Philosophical Interrogations*. New York: Holt, Rinehart, and Winston.

————. 1965. *Anselm's Discovery: A Re-examination of the Ontological Proof for God's Existence*. LaSalle, Illinois: Open Court.

————. 1967a. *A Natural Theology for Our Time*. LaSalle, Illinois: Open Court.

————. 1967b. "What Did Anselm Discover?" In John Hick, ed. *The Many-Faced Argument: Recent Studies on the Ontological Argument for the Existence of God*. New York: Macmillan.

————. 1967c. "Necessity." *Review of Metaphysics* 21: 290–296.

————. 1970. *Creative Synthesis and Philosophic Method*. LaSalle, Illinois: Open Court.

————. 1973. *Born to Sing*. Bloomington: Indiana University Press.

————. 1976. "Mysticism and Rationalistic Metaphysics." *Monist* 59: 463–469.

————. 1977. "John Hick on Logical and Ontological Necessity." *Religious Studies* 13: 155–165.

————. 1983. *Insights and Oversights of Great Thinkers*. Albany: State University of New York Press.

————. 1984a. *Creativity in American Philosophy*. Albany: State University of New York Press.

————. 1984b. *Omnipotence and Other Theological Mistakes*. Albany: State University of New York Press.

————. 1987. *Wisdom as Moderation*. Albany: State University of New York Press.

————. 1990. *The Darkness and the Light*. Albany: State University of New York Press.

————. 1991. "Ford on Whitehead's and My Philosophy." In Lewis Hahn, ed. *The Philosophy of Charles Hartshorne*. LaSalle, Illinois: Open Court.

————. 1995. "Rorty's Pragmatism and Farewell to the Age of Faith and Enlightenment." In Herman Saatkamp, ed. *Rorty & Pragmatism*. Nashville: Vanderbilt University Press.

————. 2000. *Philosophers Speak of God* (with William Reese). Amherst, New York: Humanity Books.

————. 2001. "God as Composer-Director, Enjoyer, and, in a Sense, Player of the Cosmic Drama." *Process Studies* 30: 242–260.

Hartt, Julian. 1963. "Review of *The Logic of Perfection*, by Charles Hartshorne." *Review of Metaphysics* 16: 749–769.

Haught, John. 2000. *God After Darwin*. Boulder: Westview.

Heidegger, Martin. 1959. *An Introduction to Metaphysics*. Ralph Manheim, tr. New York: Doubleday.

Herrera, R. A. 1979. *Anselm's "Proslogion": An Introduction*. Washington, DC: University Press of America.

Hick, John, ed. 1967. *The Many-Faced Argument: Recent Studies on the Ontological Argument for the Existence of God*. New York: Macmillan.

Hogg, David. 2004. *Anselm of Canterbury*. Burlington, Vermont: Ashgate.

Hubbeling, Hubertus. 1991. "Hartshorne and the Ontological Argument." In Lewis Hahn, ed. *The Philosophy of Charles Hartshorne*. LaSalle, Illinois: Open Court.

Jantzen, Grace. 1984. *God's World, God's Body*. Philadelphia: Westminster Press.

Johnson, Galen. 1977. "Hartshorne's Arguments against Empirical Evidence for Necessary Existence." *Religious Studies* 13: 175–187.

Johnson, Greg. 1998. "Process Philosophy as Postmodern Philosophy." *American Journal of Theology & Philosophy* 19: 255–273.

Johnson, J. Prescott. 1963. "The Ontological Argument in Plato." *Personalist* 44: 24–34.

Jung, Carl. 1954. *Answer to Job*. R. F. C. Hull, tr. New York: Meridian.

Kane, Robert. 1984. "The Modal Ontological Argument." *Mind* 93: 336–350.

Koyre, Alexandre. 1923. *L'Idée de Dieu dans la philosophie de S. Anselme*. Paris: J. Vrin.

Kung, Hans. 1980. *Does God Exist?* Edward Quinn, tr. New York: Doubleday.

Langtry, Bruce. 1999. "Review of Graham Oppy, *Ontological Arguments and Belief in God*." *Sophia* 36: 147–150.

Lewis, David. 1983. "Anselm and Actuality." In *Philosophical Papers*. Vol. 1. New York: Oxford University Press.

Loffler, Winfried. 1994. "Modale Versionen des ontologischen Arguments fur die Existenz Gottes." In Georg Meggle, ed. *Analyomen*. Berlin: de Gruyter.

Lomasky, Loren. 1970. "Leibniz and the Modal Argument for God's Existence." *Monist* 54: 250–269.

Lucas, Billy Joe. 1981. The Logic of Omniscience. Ph.D. dissertation. University of Texas at Austin.

———. 1997. "Review of Graham Oppy, *Ontological Arguments and Belief in God*." *International Journal for Philosophy of Religion* 41: 181–183.

———. 2003. "The Second Epistemic Way." In George Shields, ed. *Process and Analysis*. Albany: State University of New York Press.

MacIntyre, Alasdair, and Paul Ricoeur. 1969. *The Religious Significance of Atheism*. New York: Columbia University Press.

Mackie, J. L. 1976. "The Riddle of Existence." *Proceedings of the Aristotelian Society* 50: 247–265.

———. 1982. *The Miracle of Theism*. Oxford: Clarendon Press.

Makin, Stephen. 1988. "The Ontological Argument." *Philosophy* 63: 83–91.

———. 1992. "The Ontological Argument Defended." *Philosophy* 67: 247–255.

Malachowski, Alan. 2003. *Richard Rorty*. Princeton: Princeton University Press.

Malcolm, Norman. 1960. "Anselm's Ontological Arguments." *Philosophical Review* 69: 41–62.

Malin, Shimon. 2001. *Nature Loves to Hide: Quantum Physics and Reality, a Western Perspective*. Oxford: Oxford University Press.

Martin, Michael. 1990. *Atheism: A Philosophical Justification*. Philadelphia: Temple University Press.

Martin, R. M. 1984. "On the Language of Theology." In John Cobb, ed. *Existence and Actuality: Conversations with Charles Hartshorne*. Chicago: University of Chicago Press.

Matthews, Gareth. 1963. "Aquinas on Saying That God Does Not Exist." *Monist* 47: 472–477.

———. 2005. "The Ontological Argument." In William Mann, ed. *The Blackwell Guide to the Philosophy of Religion*. Oxford: Blackwell.

Maydole, Robert. 2003. "The Modal Perfection Argument for the Existence of a Supreme Being." *Philo* 6: 299–313.

McGill, Arthur. 1967. "Recent Discussions of Anselm's Argument." In John Hick, ed. *The Many-Faced Argument: Recent Studies on the Ontological Argument for the Existence of God*. New York: Macmillan.

Mesquita, Antonio. 1994. "O Argumento Ontologico em Platao." *Philosophica*: 85–109.

Millican, Peter. 2004. "The One Fatal Flaw in Anselm's Argument." *Mind* 113: 437–476.

Moore, Andrew. 2003. *Realism and Christian Faith*. Cambridge: Cambridge University Press.

Moore, G. E. 1965. "Is Existence a Predicate?" In Alvin Plantinga, ed. *The Ontological Argument: From St. Anselm to Contemporary Philosophers*. Garden City, New York: Anchor Books.

Morewedge, Parviz. 1970. "Ibn Sina (Avicenna) and Malcolm and the Ontological Argument." *Monist* 54: 234–249.

Morris, Randall. 1991. *Process Philosophy and Political Ideology*. Albany: State University of New York Press.

Morris, Thomas. 1986. *The Logic of God Incarnate*. Ithaca: Cornell University Press.

———. 1987. *Anselmian Explorations: Essays in Philosophical Theology*. Notre Dame: University of Notre Dame Press.

———. 1991. *Our Idea of God: An Introduction to Philosophical Theology*. Notre Dame: University of Notre Dame Press.

Mukerji, R. N. 2001. "The Ontological Argument and Indian Religious Thinking." *Journal of Indian Council of Philosophical Research* 18: 185–190.

Muller, Jorn. 2003. "Moglichkeit und Notwendigkeit der Existenz Gottes: Anselms ontologischer Gottesbeweis in der modallogischen Deutung von Charles Hartshorne." *Veritas* 48: 397–415.

Nakhnikian, George. 1967. "St. Anselm's Four Ontological Arguments." In W. H. Capitan, ed. *Art, Mind, and Religion*. Pittsburgh: University of Pittsburgh Press.

Nancarrow, Paul. 1995. "Realism and Anti-Realism: A Whiteheadian Response to Richard Rorty Concerning Truth, Propositions, and Practice." *Process Studies* 24: 59–75.

Nasser, Alan, and Patterson Brown. 1969. "Hartshorne's Epistemic Proof." *Australasian Journal of Philosophy* 47: 61–64.

Nelson, John. 1963. "Modal Logic and the Ontological Proof for God's Existence." *Review of Metaphysics* 17: 235–242.

Nelson, Mark. 1996. "Who Are the Best Judges of Theistic Arguments?" *Sophia* 35: 1–12.

Nietzsche, Friedrich. 1984. *Human, All Too Human.* Marion Faber, tr. Lincoln: University of Nebraska Press.

Nolan, Lawrence. 2001. "Descartes' Ontological Argument." *Stanford Encyclopedia of Philosophy* (June 18). http://plato.stanford.edu.

Nussbaum, Charles. 1994. "Did Kant Refute the Ontological Argument?" *Southwest Philosophy Review* 10: 147–156.

Oakes, Robert. 1998. "Review of Graham Oppy, *Ontological Arguments and Belief in God.*" *Faith and Philosophy* 15: 379–383.

Oppy, Graham. 1991. "Makin on the Ontological Argument." *Philosophy* 66: 106–114.

———. 1992a. "Why Semantic Innocence?" *Australasian Journal of Philosophy* 70: 445–454.

———. 1992b. "Semantics for Propositional Attitude Ascriptions." *Philosophical Studies* 67: 1–18.

———. 1992c. "Is God Good by Definition?" *Religious Studies* 28: 467–474.

———. 1993a. "Makin's Ontological Argument (Again)." *Philosophy* 68: 234–239.

———. 1993b. "Modal Theistic Arguments." *Sophia* 32: 17–24.

———. 1994. "Weak Agnosticism Defended." *International Journal for Philosophy of Religion* 36: 147–167.

———. 1995. *Ontological Arguments and Belief in God.* Cambridge: Cambridge University Press.

———. 1996. "Godelian Ontological Arguments." *Analysis* 56: 226–230.

———. 1998. "Judging Theistic Arguments." *Sophia* 37: 30–43.

———. 2001. "Reply to Langtry." *Sophia* 40: 73–80.

———. 2003. "The Devilish Complexities of Divine Simplicity." *Philo* 6: 10–22.

Oppy, Graham, and Michael Almeida. 2003. "Sceptical Theism and Evidential Arguments from Evil." *Australasian Journal of Philosophy* 81: 496–516.

Oppy, Graham, F. Jackson, and M. Smith. 1994. "Minimalism and Truth Aptness." *Mind* 103: 287–302.

Oppy, Graham, and John O'Leary-Hawthorne. 1997. "Minimalism and Truth." *Nous* 31: 170–196.

Pailin, David. 1968. "Some Comments on Hartshorne's Presentation of the Ontological Argument." *Religious Studies* 4: 103–122.

Paulson, David. 1984. "The Logically Possible, the Ontologically Possible, and Ontological Proofs for God's Existence." *International Journal for Philosophy of Religion* 16: 41–50.

Peikoff, Leonard. 1984. "Platonism's Inference from Logic to God." *International Studies in Philosophy* 16: 25–34.

Pinnock, Clark, ed. 1994. *The Openness of God: A Biblical Challenge to the Traditional Understanding of God.* Downers Grove, Illinois: InterVarsity Press.

Plantinga, Alvin, ed. 1965. *The Ontological Argument: From St. Anselm to Contemporary Philosophers.* Garden City, New York: Anchor Books.

———. 1967. *God and Other Minds.* Ithaca: Cornell University Press.

———. 1974. *The Nature of Necessity.* Oxford: Clarendon Press.

———. 1980. *Does God Have a Nature?* Milwaukee: Marquette University Press.

————. 2003. *Essays in the Metaphysics of Modality*. Oxford: Oxford University Press.

Popper, Karl. 1963. "On the Status of Science and Metaphysics." In *Conjectures and Refutations*. London: Routledge.

Pratt, Douglas. 2002. *Relational Deity: Hartshorne and Macquarrie on God*. Lanham, Maryland: University Press of America.

Pruss, Alexander. 2001. "Sankara's Principle and Two Ontomystical Arguments." *International Journal for Philosophy of Religion* 49: 111–120.

Purtill, Richard. 1966. "Hartshorne's Modal Proof." *Journal of Philosophy* 63: 397–409.

————. 1975. "Three Ontological Arguments." *International Journal for Philosophy of Religion* 6: 102–110.

Quine, W. V. O. 1963. *From a Logical Point of View*. New York: Harper and Row.

Randall, John Herman. 1960. *Aristotle*. New York: Columbia University Press.

Rescher, Nicholas. 1960. "A Ninth-Century Arabic Logician on: Is Existence a Predicate?" *Journal of the History of Ideas* 21: 428–430.

Richman, Robert. 1958. "The Ontological Proof of the Devil." *Philosophical Studies* (Minnesota) 9: 63–64.

Rogers, Katherin. 1997a. *The Anselmian Approach to God and Creation*. Lewiston, New York: Edwin Mellen Press.

————. 1997b. *The Neoplatonic Metaphysics and Epistemology of Anselm of Canterbury*. Lewiston, New York: Edwin Mellen Press.

————. 2000. *Perfect Being Theology*. Edinburgh: Edinburgh University Press.

————. 2003. "Philosophy of Religion." In Leemon McHenry, ed. *Reflections on Philosophy: Introductory Essays*. New York: Longman.

Rorty, Richard. 1961. "Pragmatism, Categories, and Language." *Philosophical Review* 70: 197–223.

————. 1963a. "Matter and Event." In Ernan McMullin, ed. *The Concept of Matter*. Notre Dame: Notre Dame University Press.

————. 1963b. "Review of *Understanding Whitehead*, by Victor Lowe." *Journal of Philosophy* 60 (April 25): 246–251.

————. 1963c. "Comments on Professor Hartshorne's Paper." *Journal of Philosophy* 60 (Oct. 10): 606–608.

————. 1963d. "The Subjectivist Principle and the Linguistic Turn." In George Kline, ed. *Alfred North Whitehead: Essays on His Philosophy*. Englewood Cliffs, New Jersey: Prentice-Hall.

————. 1967. "Relations, Internal and External." *Encyclopedia of Philosophy*. New York: Macmillan.

————. 1979. *Philosophy and the Mirror of Nature*. Princeton: Princeton University Press.

————. 1994. "Does Academic Freedom Have Philosophical Presuppositions?" *Academe* 80 (Nov.): 52–63.

————. 1995. "Response to Charles Hartshorne." In Herman Saatkamp, ed. *Rorty & Pragmatism*. Nashville: Vanderbilt University Press.

————. 1998. *Truth and Progress: Philosophical Papers*. Vol. 3. Cambridge: Cambridge University Press.

————. 1999. *Philosophy and Social Hope*. New York: Penguin.

———. 2000. "Response to Michael Williams." In Robert Brandom, ed. *Rorty and His Critics.* Oxford: Blackwell.

———. 2002. "Cultural Politics and the Question of the Existence of God." In Nancy Frankenberry, ed. *Radical Interpretation in Religion.* New York: Cambridge University Press.

———. 2003. "Religion in the Public Square: A Reconsideration." *Journal of Religious Ethics* 31: 141–149.

———. 2005. *The Future of Religion.* New York: Columbia University Press.

Ross, James. 1977. "An Impasse on Competing Descriptions of God." *International Journal for Philosophy of Religion* 8: 233–249.

Rousseau, Edward. 1980. "St. Anselm and St. Thomas – A Reconsideration." *New Scholasticism* 54: 1–24.

Salmon, Nathan. 1987. "Existence." In J. Tomberlin, ed. *Philosophical Perspectives.* Vol. 1. Atascadero, California: Ridgeview.

Schmidt, Thomas. Forthcoming. "Reasonable Pluralism, Justified Beliefs, and Religious Faith in a Pluralist Society."

Schnepf, Robert. 1998. "Sein als Ereignis: Zu einigen Voraussetzungen des Gottes-beweises bei Anselm von Canterbury." *Patristica et Mediaevalia* 19: 3–22.

Schrimpf, Gangolf. 1994. *Anselm von Canterbury, Proslogion II–IV.* Frankfurt: Knecht.

Shields, George. 2003. "Introduction: On the Interface of Analytic and Process Philosophy." In George Shields, ed. *Process and Analysis.* Albany: State University of New York Press.

Shields, George, and Donald Viney. 2003. "The Logic of Future Contingents." In George Shields, ed. *Process and Analysis.* Albany: State University of New York Press.

Smith, John. 1968. *Experience and God.* Oxford: Oxford University Press.

———. 1984. "Some Aspects of Hartshorne's Treatment of Anselm." In John Cobb, ed. *Existence and Actuality: Conversations with Charles Hartshorne.* Chicago: University of Chicago Press.

Sontag, Frederick. 1967. "The Meaning of 'Argument' in Anselm's Ontological Proof." *Journal of Philosophy* 64: 459–486.

Stearns, J. Brenton. 1970. "Anselm and the Two-Argument Hypothesis." *Monist* 54: 221–233.

Steinitz, Yuval. 1994. "Necessary Beings." *American Philosophical Quarterly* 31: 177–182.

Stolz, Anselm. 1967. "Anselm's Theology in the *Proslogion.*" In John Hick, ed. *The Many-Faced Argument: Recent Studies on the Ontological Argument for the Existence of God.* New York: Macmillan.

Taliaferro, Charles. 1997. "Review of Graham Oppy, *Ontological Arguments and Belief in God.*" *Australasian Journal of Philosophy* 75: 553–555.

Taylor, Mark. 1977. "*Itinerarium Mentis in Deum*: Hegel's Proofs of God's Existence." *The Journal of Religion* 57: 211–231.

———. 1980. *Journeys to Selfhood: Hegel and Kierkegaard.* Berkeley: University of California Press.

———. 1982. *Deconstructing Theology.* New York: Crossroad.

———. 1984. *Erring: A Postmodern A/theology*. Chicago: University of Chicago Press.

———. 1987. *Altarity*. Chicago: University of Chicago Press.

———. 1990. *Tears*. Albany: State University of New York Press.

———. 1992. *Disfiguring: Art, Architecture, Religion*. Chicago: University of Chicago Press.

———. 1993. *nOts*. Chicago: University of Chicago Press.

———. 1997. *Hiding*. Chicago: University of Chicago Press.

———. 1999a. *About Religion: Economies of Faith in Virtual Culture*. Chicago: University of Chicago Press.

———. 1999b. *The Picture in Question*. Chicago: University of Chicago Press.

Tillich, Paul. 1964. *Theology of Culture*. Robert Kimball, tr. New York: Oxford University Press.

Tomanek, Roman. 1995. "Saint Anselm's Argument in the Formalized Version of Charles Hartshorne." *Studia Philosophiae Christianae* 31: 99–104.

Tooley, Michael. 1981. "Plantinga's Defense of the Ontological Argument." *Mind* 90: 422–427.

Towne, Edgar. 1997. *Two Types of New Theism: Knowledge of God in the Thought of Paul Tillich and Charles Hartshorne*. New York: Peter Lang.

———. 1999. "Semantics and Hartshorne's Dipolar Theism." *Process Studies* 28: 231–254.

Van Inwagen, Peter. 1998. "Arguments for God's Existence: Ontological Arguments." In Brian Davies, ed. *Philosophy of Religion*. Washington, DC: Georgetown University Press.

Vaught, Carl. 1972. "Hartshorne's Ontological Argument: An Instance of Misplaced Concreteness." *International Journal for Philosophy of Religion* 3: 18–34.

Viney, Donald. 1985. *Charles Hartshorne and the Existence of God*. Albany: State University of New York Press.

———. 1998. "The Varieties of Theism and the Openness of God: Charles Hartshorne and Free Will Theism." *Personalist Forum* 14: 199–238.

———. 2003. "Charles Hartshorne." In Leemon McHenry, ed. *American Philosophers before 1950*. Farmington Hills, Michigan: Thomson Learning.

———. 2004. "Process Theism." *Stanford Encyclopedia of Philosophy* (July 29). http://plato.stanford.edu.

Weidemann, Hermann. 2004. "Anselm und die Insel: Das ontologische Argument im Spiegel surrealistischer Kunst." *Archiv fuer Geschichte der Philosophie* 86: 1–20.

Whitehead, Alfred North. 1961. *Adventures of Ideas*. New York: Macmillan.

———. 1978. *Process and Reality*. Corrected edition. New York: Free Press.

Wiehl, Reiner. 1991. "Hartshorne's Panpsychism." In Lewis Hahn, ed. *The Philosophy of Charles Hartshorne*. LaSalle, Illinois: Open Court.

Wierenga, Edward. 1998. "Review of Graham Oppy, *Ontological Arguments and Belief in God*." *Review of Metaphysics* 52: 163–164.

Wild, John. 1950. "The Divine Existence: An Answer to Mr. Hartshorne." *Review of Metaphysics* 4: 61–84.

Williams, Christopher. 1981. *What Is Existence?* Oxford: Oxford University Press.

Wordsworth, William. 1981. *Poetical Works*. Oxford: Oxford University Press.

Index

Made in the USA
Middletown, DE
26 May 2023

31216272R00109